Eerie Iowa

Eerie Iowa

Michael McCarty & Bruce Walters

The History Press

Published by The History Press
An imprint of Arcadia Publishing
Charleston, SC
www.historypress.com

First published 2025

Manufactured in the United States

ISBN 9781467158503

Library of Congress Control Number: 2025941520

Dedicated to the "Amazing Kreskin"
(George J. Kresge, January 12, 1935–December 10, 2024).
Thanks for writing the introductions
to Ghosts of the Quad Cities *and* Eerie Quad Cities, *as well as*
and co-writing Conversations with Kreskin *with Michael McCarty.*
You will always be amazing in our hearts.

And to Living Local *(WHBF Channel 4) producers and co-hosts*
Tristan Tapscott and Brandy Auterson, camera person Angie Scott
and the other talented people on the show. Many thanks for supporting and
broadcasting programs about our books Ghosts of the Quad Cities,
Eerie Quad Cities *and* Quad Cities Beer: A History.

CONTENTS

FOREWORD

Minda Powers-Douglas ready for ghost hunting. *Courtesy of Minda Powers-Douglas.*

Iowa is weird, and that is wonderful. I mean that literally. There are so many places in Iowa that contain so much wonder—things that are unexpectedly great, things that are extraordinary.

It's no secret that I love eerie stuff. After all, I do run my own ghost tour business. It's a love I have had since I was a kid. I read every ghost story I could get my hands on—truth or fiction—and watched every scary movie my parents allowed. The older I got, the more I learned about haunted places around the country and even a few in the area, usually by word of mouth. In the 1980s, books about local hauntings weren't exactly lining the shelves. For instance, the *one* book I found mentioned only two hauntings in my hometown of Moline: a pointing ghost on what's now Avenue of the Cities and a shoveling skeleton in someone's yard. Talk about *disappointing*! Ghost fans today are lucky to have books like *Ghosts of the Quad Cities* (by Michael McCarty and Mark McLaughlin), *Eerie Quad Cities* (by Michael McCarty and John Brassard Jr.) and now *Eerie Iowa* (by Michael McCarty and Bruce Walters).

In recent years, I've been fortunate enough to participate in paranormal investigations at haunted locations, both local and beyond. Young me from years ago would have freaked out if she knew she would eventually be

The *Field of Dreams* baseball field from the cornfield. *Courtesy Bruce Walters.*

going on real ghost hunts *and* experiencing actual paranormal activity. I had dreamed of it for years. I went on every ghost tour I could and wandered around places said to be haunted. To my dismay, I never felt, saw or heard a thing. That wouldn't happen until I was in my forties. Good thing forty is the new thirty because I've got things to do!

In 2019, I started QC Haunts & History. I offer outdoor walking tours in downtown Rock Island, and in the fall of 2024, I added a tour in the historic Village of East Davenport, right across the Mississippi River. Ever since I began my tour business, I've met many people who share my interest in the paranormal—people who've lived in haunted houses, paranormal investigators, psychic mediums and people who want to know more about what's beyond the here and now. Some of them became tour guides or volunteers. Every one of them is greatly appreciated, probably more than they know. Several of us have gone on paranormal investigations in both Iowa and Illinois. During those events, we observed and encountered spirits that communicated through the equipment we used or one or more of the psychic mediums. If that's not a wonder, I don't know what it is.

I've been to several of the places listed in this book. I've been to the Black Angel of Iowa City and survived to tell the tale. I've visited the Field of

Dreams, although no ghosts came out of the cornfield. I know all about Vice Lord John Looney and his evil reign during the early 1900s, as he's featured in my "Gangsters & Ghosts" tour.

I hope you enjoy these stories. Visit the locations if you can. Experience the weird and embrace the wonderful. Explore *Eerie Iowa*. You won't regret it.

—MINDA POWERS-DOUGLAS

PREFACE

Iowa, the heart of the heartland, is an endless stretch of cornfields, barns and silos under a vast country sky. The state also boasts metropolitan cities with more than 100,000 residents, wind turbines, Friday night football and bustling county and state fairs. It is the home of John Wayne, Caitlin Clark, *Field of Dreams* and *The Bridges of Madison County*.

But there's another Iowa—a darker reflection where the air is thick with secrets and the soil itself seems to whisper of things long forgotten. You'll find eerie cemeteries tucked behind old country churches, with tombstones weathered by time and a past that goes deeper than the plots of their dead.

Buckle up. The next time you find yourself cruising down I-80, you might think twice before taking that detour into a small town or turning down a dusty gravel road—because you are about to enter *Eerie Iowa*.

I owe thanks to all the fans who supported my spooky Iowa books: *Ghosts of the Quad Cities* and *Eerie Quad Cities*. And to Bruce for journeying all over the Hawkeye State to take photos, draw, research and write.

I hope everyone will enjoy this dark ride with *Eerie Iowa* too.

—MICHAEL

Photo and artwork by Bruce Walters.

Above: Michael McCarty and Bruce Walters at the *Ghosts of the Quad Cities* book signing, Barnes & Noble, Northpark Mall. *Courtesy Cindy McCarty.*

Opposite: Abandoned Davenport barn with a perching vulture. *Courtesy Michael McCarty.*

Overhead, Iowa is a quilt of green patches of cornfields stitched together by highways that connect its 934 cities. It's a picturesque Grant Wood painting of rural America.

But from the ground, these fields feel very different. If you've ever walked through endless rows of corn, you'll know viscerally how eerie and disorienting they can be. The towering stalks create narrow corridors of vegetation, limiting what can be seen or heard. When the wind stirs the stalks, it feels as if something is moving in the field just out of sight. In *Field of Dreams*, the ghosts of long-dead baseball players emerge not from a graveyard, but from the corn itself.

The word *eerie* shares certain qualities with *mystery*—both involve an awareness of the unknown. But *eeriness* is unsettling. A drive along a lonely rural road at dusk, with fields stretching endlessly to the horizon, is a liminal experience. These spaces in Iowa capture a haunting quiet—a sense of being suspended between past and present, civilization and wilderness, the seen and the unseen.

Sigmund Freud explored eeriness in his 1919 essay "The Uncanny" ("Das Unheimliche"). He described it as something both familiar and unfamiliar—an experience where what was hidden or repressed suddenly comes to light. These moments provoke unease precisely because they disturb our sense of the ordinary.

Carl Jung's work on myths and symbols often intersects with the eerie. He believed that symbols emerge from the unconscious, expressing deep fears, desires or unresolved tensions. Archetypes like the trickster or shadow figure in myths embody this unsettling, mysterious quality. Jung and Freud offer a rich framework for understanding why certain places, images or feelings evoke a deep sense of unease.

Don't simply follow the path to the places Michael and I have written about. Open the door you haven't dared to open—until now.

—BRUCE

ACKNOWLEDGEMENTS

My lovely wife, Cindy McCarty; my good friend and writing partner Bruce Walters; Bruce Cook; Raymond Congrove; Scott Faust; the McCartys; the Hultings; the Leonards; Mel Piff; Jack; Camilla Bowman; Holly Zaldivar; Nancy Johnston; Brian Kilgore; Joan Mauch; the Beach Party Zombies; the memory of my parents, Bev and Gerald; Yeti; the memory of Kitty and Latte; and all my family and friends and fans. You are the reason I keep writing.

—Michael

My wonderful wife, Laurie, and my three children, Emile, Justin and Andrew. Also thanks to my co-pilots during the Iowa adventures: Al Bieg, my brother Ed and my co-writer, Michael McCarty.

—Bruce

We would also like to thank The History Press, Lawson Jenkins, Benjamin Gibson, Holly Zaldivar, Peg Rounds and Whispering Souls Paranormal, Dave and Julie Thompson, Doug Smith, Davenport Iowa History on Facebook, Richard-Sloane Special Collection of the Davenport Library, Rock Island Library, Penni Steen and Skellington

Manor, Chad Lewis, Bret Grimes, Cammie and Randy Pohl, Minda Powers-Douglas, Bill Douglas, Andrew Walters, Neoma Finn, Kelly and Tammy Rundle, Fourth Wall Films, Scott Naumann, Clare Tobin, Jolene Harvey, Veronique Fernandez, Shannon Trimble, Philip Force, Max Collins, Roger Ruthhart, the Putnam Museum, Linda Cook, Jonathan Turner, Hauberg Estate, the Source Bookstore, Lynn Herington and Barnes & Noble, Cheri Day and Obsidian & Sage, the Dark Side of Davenport tours, the Quad Cities Convention and Visitors Bureau, the Midwest Writing Center, the German American Heritage Center, Scott Community College, Nick Vulich, Marlena Midnite, Blake Powell, *Midnite Mausoleum*, Mark Manuel and BIG 106 FM, *Living Local*, *River Cities Reader*, WHBF and KWQC and the Quad Cities for being so supportive of our work. Of course, we thank Chad Rhoad, our fearless acquisitions editor, who guided us through the winding course of getting this book published.

—MICHAEL AND BRUCE

IOWA'S EERIE PAST

1803 Louisiana Territory: Thomas Jefferson purchases the Louisiana Territory from France, doubling the size of the United States, including present-day Iowa.

1833 Iowa Territory: The Black Hawk Purchase opens land in Iowa to settlers. About forty to fifty settlers reside in Iowa, along with an estimated fifteen thousand Native Americans at this time.

1846 Iowa becomes the twenty-ninth state, entering the Union as a free state. Article I, Section 1 of its constitution begins, "There shall be neither slavery nor involuntary servitude in this state."

1854 Muscatine: Samuel Clemens works at the *Muscatine Journal*. As Mark Twain, his writings have elements of the uncanny, especially in relation to the Mississippi River and small towns along its banks.

1857 Dubuque: The Mathias Ham House is built and becomes known as one of Iowa's most haunted houses.

1861 Mount Pleasant: Iowa's first mental institution, Mount Pleasant Insane Asylum, opens.

1862 Davenport: The Germania House is built as an inn for immigrants. It is later said to be haunted by Otto Koechert, who died in 1891.

Inside the gristmill at Wild Cat Den. *Courtesy Bruce Walters.*

1871 Corydon: Jesse James and his gang rob Obocock Bank. Two years later, they rob a train in Adair.

1874 Davenport: Reverend Jacob Gass uncovers slate tablets with mysterious symbols—known internationally as the Davenport Tablets.

1879 Estherville: A massive meteorite fall occurs on May 10, described as a loud, eerie explosion. It is the largest observed meteorite fall in North America.

1883 Winterset: The Roseman Covered Bridge is built and gains a haunted reputation after an escaped prisoner trapped on the bridge vanishes.

1895 Davenport: D.D. Palmer performs the first chiropractic adjustment, claiming knowledge received during a séance.

1897 Sioux City: Mysterious sightings of a UFO are first seen in Sioux City. It is sighted continuously as it crosses the entire state.

1903 Van Meter: A flying monster terrorizes the town in what becomes known as the "Van Meter Visitor" encounter.

1903 Lake Okoboji: A lake monster is sighted from a boat. The Keokuk Sea Monster appears ten years later.

1912 Villisca: Eight people, including six children, are murdered in their beds with an axe. The case remains unsolved.

1912 Iowa City: The eerie Black Angel statue arrives at Oakland Cemetery by flatcar.

1915 Cresco: The Cresco Opera House opens. Spectral vaudeville performers are seen on stage.

1920 Council Bluffs: The Ruth Anne Dodge Memorial (Black Angel) is completed by Daniel Chester French and modeled after Audrey Munson.

1922 Columbus Junction: The haunted Swinging Bridge is built, replacing an earlier bridge that had been condemned.

1928 West Branch: Herbert Hoover is elected the thirty-first U.S. president. A mysterious seven-foot statue of the goddess Isis is later installed on a winding pathway between Hoover's Presidential Library and the small house where he was born in 1874.

1928 Earling: Emma Schmidt undergoes a twenty-eight-day exorcism at the Convent of the Franciscan Sisters. It becomes one of the most documented American exorcisms and reportedly inspired *The Exorcist.*

1929 Council Bluffs: Jake Bird begins serving time in the notorious Squirrel Cage Jail for an axe assault at Carter Lake. When later convicted of multiple axe murders, he utters his deadly curse.

1933 Dexter: Bonnie and Clyde and their gang hide in the abandoned Dexfield amusement park. In a shootout with law enforcement, the gang members are either killed or wounded, some severely.

1936 Iowa City: The Iowa Writers' Workshop is established. Alumni include John Irving, Rita Dove, Flannery O'Connor, W.P. Kinsella, Joe Haldeman and Carmen Maria Machado. Kurt Vonnegut would teach at the workshop from 1965 to 1967, writing *Cat's Cradle* and starting *Slaughterhouse-Five.*

1950 Davenport: A fire at St. Elizabeth's Hospital claims the lives of forty psychiatric patients and one nurse. The tragic event remains one of Iowa's deadliest institutional disasters.

1951 Davenport: Helen Van Dale, the "Queen of the Looney Underworld," is buried in an unmarked grave at Fairmount Cemetery. Her testimony helped convict gangster John Looney, who is also buried in an unmarked grave.

1959 Clear Lake: On February 3, musicians Buddy Holly, Ritchie Valens and The Big Bopper die in a plane crash outside Clear Lake. The event becomes known as the "Day the Music Died."

1964–68 Waterloo/Anamosa: John Wayne Gacy manages several Kentucky Fried Chicken restaurants in Waterloo. In 1968, he is sent to the Anamosa State Penitentiary.

1965 Davenport: The B.J. and Mabel H. Palmer Memorial Trust donates more than two thousand objects to the Putnam Museum, including the mummy and sarcophagus of Isis Neferit.

1989 Dyersville: *Field of Dreams* is released. The film tells of an Iowa farmer who builds a baseball field where the ghosts of legendary players appear. Shoeless Joe Jackson becomes a symbol of redemption and mystery.

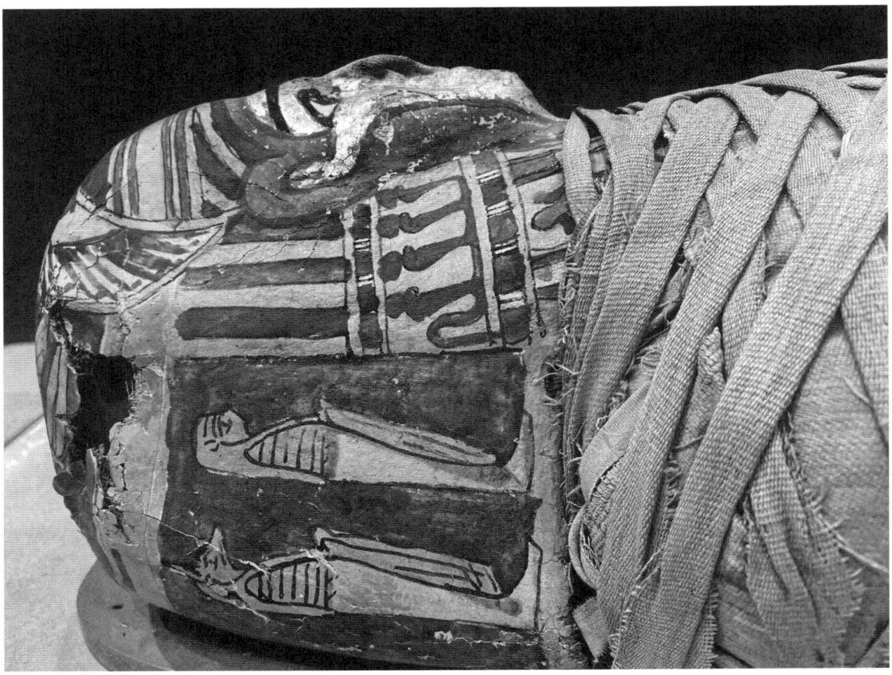

The mummy sarcophagus at the Putnam Museum and Science Center. *Courtesy Bruce Walters.*

Wind turbine. *Courtesy Bruce Walters.*

1995 Winterset: *The Bridges of Madison County*, based on the novel by Iowan Robert James Waller, is released. Filming locations include the haunted Roseman Covered Bridge.

2233 Riverside: Captain James T. Kirk of the USS *Enterprise* will be born on March 22, 2233. William Shatner, who portrayed Kirk, shares the same birthday, though 302 years before.

Part I

CURIOUS CREATURES, UFOs AND STRANGE HAPPENINGS

The Van Meter Visitor

In 1903, as autumn settled in at the end of September and the beginning of October, the residents of Van Meter witnessed a winged creature—a mysterious monster flying around, leaping from house to house, striking terror throughout the small town. The creepy cryptid has come to be known as the Van Meter Visitor.

Coauthor Chad Lewis wrote *The Van Meter Visitor: A True and Mysterious Encounter with the Unknown*. Mr. Lewis has written numerous books about legends and supernatural occurrences in the Midwest. He described the Van Meter Visitor, reporting, "A giant half-human half-bat creature was spotted in the small town of Van Meter. Witnesses described it as being over 8 feet tall with huge leathery wings like a bat. On the top of its head was a blunt horn that it could project light out of. We do not have any idea what color it was, as most of the sightings were in the pitch-black darkness of night."

Mr. Lewis continued, "The original 1903 sightings occurred over five nights. As far as we know only a couple of people spotted it each night. However, by the last night dozens of armed men blasted at the creatures (now there were two of them—one was much smaller as though it was an offspring or perhaps a female gender of the species). So overall several dozen people caught a glimpse of this terrifying beast."

The Van Meter Visitor, a winged monster that terrorized a small town. *Courtesy Bruce Walters.*

In *Secret Iowa*, Megan Bannister wrote, "Over the next few days, several of the community's most well-respected citizens reported seeing the same figure flying through the sky. All reported that it appeared to be half human and half animal with gigantic, smooth wings like a bat."

Nick Vulich, in his book *Gruesome Iowa*, included these witness accounts:

> *Peter Dunne, a cashier at the bank, heard a curious scratching sound coming from around the corner from the bank, then saw a blinding light. He grabbed his shotgun and fired at it. The next morning, he found imprints from three-toe feet behind the bank....*
>
> *Sidney Gregg watched the creature fly away. He said it moved around like a kangaroo, leaping and flapping its large featherless wings....*
>
> *J.L. Pratt, Jr. worked at the tile plant on the northwest edge of town. About 1 a.m. a noise erupted from inside of the abandoned mine. It "sounded like Satan and a band of imps were coming forth for battle." Two winged monsters emerged from the mine, with giant horns in the center of their heads blaring light. There was a big one and a small one....*
>
> *Dr. O.V. White had rooms over the hardware store. He heard a rasping sound and peered out the window, revolver in hand. He watched a creature climb down a telephone pole, using its beak-like third arm. Once on the ground, it leaped around using its feathers to propel itself around.*

Van Meter, Iowa, 2024. *Courtesy Bruce Walters.*

Some dismissed the Van Meter Visitor as mass hysteria. Chad Lewis explained:

> *The idea that Van Meter was nothing more than another case of mass hysteria does bear some consideration. I suppose it is possible that events which started with a simple light in the sky could, within days, blossom into a giant eight-foot bat that flies around the town with a built-in light while spewing out a mysterious memory-erasing odor.*
>
> *There are several aspects of these events I believe concretely invalidate the theory of mass hysteria in the Van Meter case. One of the main hallmarks of mass hysteria involves a sudden onset of irrational thinking and/or behavior accompanied by inexplicable symptoms of illness (like getting sick from a phantom gasser). But outside of O.V. White's sudden inability to recall key elements of his night, no other physical or psychological symptoms were reported by any of the witnesses, making it highly improbable that the events in Van Meter were nothing more than mass hysteria.*

Mr. Lewis noted:

> *There is also the inclusion of physical evidence in the form of the plaster casts that were allegedly taken of the mysterious three-toed beast. While the mind can easily conjure up hallucinations, misidentifications, and complete common sense-destroying panic, being able to mentally manifest actual footprints is a bit more far-fetched. That is not to say that the witnesses, after believing that they had just encountered something supernatural, could easily "see" what they wanted to in a normal set of footprints, much like seeing shapes and figures in clouds. To find evidence of this wishful thinking happening, all one needs to do is look at the thousands of "ghost" photos online where every strange shadow of light or twisted tree branch is suddenly construed as the outline of a vengeful spirit. Perhaps Mr. Dunn felt a bit foolish by his actions and used the footprints to help justify why he shot out the front window of the bank. But until more information on the event surfaces or someone discovers a strange set of plaster-cast footprints in their attic, we may never know the real truth behind what happened in 1903. I think it is safe to say, however, that mass hysteria was not the culprit.*

Mr. Lewis, in his work *The Van Meter Visitor*, discussed the story of a winged creature that fed on various Indian tribes. Nick Vulich addressed the same issue and said that in "Perry Armstrong's *The Piasa or The Devil Among the Indians* (1887), Piasa meant 'bird that devoured men.' Indian folklore could have played a similar role in the Van Meter Visitor."

"Similar to so many other legends in America," Mr. Lewis said, "It is hard to fathom that the residents of Van Meter were not aware of previous legends of flying creatures from the indigenous peoples. To what extent this shaped their beliefs….I am not sure—nothing of the sort was mentioned in the reports."

The townsfolk of Van Meter even shot at the creepy winged creature several times with no effect. Chad Lewis explained:

> *Whatever this thing was it seemed to be impervious to weapons. Dr. Alcott was the first to take aim at this creature. It was said that he fired at the monster 5 times from close range, and it had no effect at all. The very next night, the bank manager blasted out the front window of the bank while trying to kill the beast. His shotgun filled with buckshot seemed to have missed the creature or it did no visible damage. The following night O.V. White took deliberate aim at the monster as it slept, on a telephone pole. His bullet also appeared to do nothing except to wake the monster from its slumber as it released a strange odor that erased Mr. White's memory of anything else that evening.*
>
> *The last night of sighting resembled a scene straight out of a Wild West Movie. Dozens of armed factory workers gathered near the suspected entrance of this beast. When the monster returned from its nightly terror flight through the town (again with the smaller version) the men shot it with everything they had. Newspapers claimed that they fired so many rounds at the beasts, "they could have sunk the Spanish fleet." Outside of letting out some monstrous growls from the beasts, the bullets were all but worthless.*

Some speculate that the Van Meter Visitor was a demonic creature; others say it was a curious cryptid. There is even one theory that it was an escaped animal, but Mr. Lewis doesn't buy that one. "At the time of the encounters, several popular circuses including the Orton Family circus had their winter quarters in the region around Van Meter," he said. "They would have kept all their exotic menagerie of beasts there. Although I personally do not subscribe to the idea that the visitor was a mistaken circus animal, we did want to cover all the bases and one possibility is that in the darkness of night, people…mistakenly confused a circus animal for a giant-winged humanoid. This does show that in order to really research and explore this legend, we left no stone unturned."

Even the demise of the Van Meter Visitor is divided. The one detail everyone agreed on is that the townsfolk banded together to trap the monster inside an abandoned coal mine. One account says they barricaded the entrance.

In *Secret Iowa*, Megan Bannister explored the end of the creatures in the coal mine: "There they encountered the first creature along with another smaller version. The beasts emitted horrible noises. Then in the blink of an eye, the creatures disappeared, never to be seen again."

Nick Vulich wrote in *Gruesome Iowa*, "What's unusual about the Van Meter creature is it manifested itself for four or five days and then was gone." More than a century later, the Van Meter Visitor mystery still has yet to be explained.

Every September since 2013, the town celebrates the strange and spooky legend with the Van Meter Visitor Festival (https://www.facebook.com/vanmetervisitorfestival).

Where: Van Meter.

Dogman of Cedar Rapids

In July 2014, a teenage boy around seventeen years old was sucked into a storm drain in Cedar Rapids. "The Cedar Rapids Police Department did a search and rescue trying to find him. As the day wore on and they were having less and less luck, they realized that it was quickly becoming a recovery, not a search and rescue. They called in reinforcement from Lane County," reported Neoma Finn, who is the editor of the YouTube channel "Dixie Cryptid." Finn continued:

> *The Lane County officer who had the experience was not in his normal territory. This is Mohawk Park near the Quaker Oaks factory on the Cedar River; 380 runs parallel to it. To the north, you've got, I think it's Cedar Lake. He was headed to the dam hoping to possibly find a body floating in the lake or caught in the dam.*

The Dogman of Cedar Rapids. *Courtesy Bruce Walters.*

He got out of his cruiser, and he began walking. There's lots of bike paths and footpaths, and he was walking along that area when he happened to notice a set of taillights. Red taillights up ahead. What he didn't know, because this was not his jurisdiction, was that there was no road there. So, he's walking along, the taillights disappear. He gives them no other thought. He's walking along, and all of the sudden he hears a noise. Flips his flashlight over, and he realizes that the red taillights are red eyes, and he is face to face with an eight-foot-tall creature with long ears, a snout, more teeth in his mouth than it should have, and it's growling at him. He pulled his Glock.

They stared at each other for a few minutes. The creature turned and walked away. He says there will never be an official report on this because he'd would have probably lost his job.

Is there a difference between a dogman and the traditional werewolf? "The Loup-garou (French for werewolf or lycanthrope) history begins in France and Germany," said Neoma Finn. "That's where the legend comes from. A lot of people believed that what they were seeing was a dogman. In their creative minds, they made them something that transforms from human to a wolf. 'Even a man whose pure heart and says his prayers by night.' That's all curse, yeah, nothing like that."

Finn continued, "With a werewolf, which is a legend that supposedly can change back and forth from human to wolf, and with the dogman, is a species of animal that does not change. It's born this way. It grows up this way as a Dire Wolf." The dire wolf roamed the earth 5.7 million years ago. It was a close relative of the modern wolf, but bigger and stronger.

Ms. Finn said that people have theorized that the dogman going from moving on all four to standing in an upright position causes the joints to pop, adding to the legend of the werewolf. When hearing the crackling cartilage, people thought it was a transformation from man to beast.

Where: Mohawk City Park, 100 J Avenue Northeast, Cedar Rapids.

Bigfoot in Iowa

In *Eerie Quad Cities*, Bigfoot is described as "a giant creature. It walks on two legs and shows the intelligence of a man, yet exhibits the enormous strength of an ape."

According to the folklore of many Native American tribes throughout the United States and Canada, as European settlers pushed west across the United States, they also began to have encounters with the strange, hairy being.

According to testimonials given to the Bigfoot Field Researchers Organization (BFRO), the creature has been spotted in Iowa seventy-eight times. Since 1995, the goal of BFRO has been to study the Bigfoot phenomenon by collecting as much information and empirical evidence about the creature as possible.

Bigfoot reports, according to BFRO, identify the following Iowa counties as places where Bigfoot has been seen: Boone, Buchanan, Chickasaw, Clayton, Dallas, Decatur, Delaware, Dickinson, Dubuque, Fayette, Floyd, Franklin, Fremont, Greene, Hardin, Humboldt, Jasper, Jefferson, Johnson, Keokuk, Lee, Madison, Mahska, Marion, Monroe, Polk, Pottawatta, Sac, Scott, Warren, Washington, Winneshiek and Woodbury.

There are three different accounts of Bigfoot sightings in the Quad Cities in *Eerie Quad Cities*. One is an 1869 report issued from the area near East Davenport and Bettendorf. Another comes from a group of young campers by the Wapsipinicon River. There is also a brief mention of two additional cases, one in Hampton, Illinois, and another in Eldridge, Iowa, in 1981.

Eldridge

Neoma Finn, the editor of the YouTube channel "Dixie Cryptid," heard about the Eldridge, Iowa newspaper encounter while listening to a podcast called *Sasquatch Chronicles*, hosted by Wes Germer:

> *Guests tell him their encounter stories. It gives them a place to talk about it, where they feel safe and comfortable. They're not going to be made fun of. And this guy comes on and starts talking about when he was a 13-year-old. It was seven or eight years ago. I may not have every detail correct, but this is what I remember him saying:*
>
> *It was wintertime. He was already not happy with being a paper boy. His dad, being an old-fashioned Midwestern father, was like, "Nope, you're going to get out there and you're going to do this job." It had snowed the night before and it was cold. Temperatures had dropped. He gets to the drop-off site, he cuts open the bundle, and he wraps up his papers, as he's supposed to do, and he heads out to deliver papers. And he*

Bigfoot in Eldridge. *Courtesy Bruce Walters.*

goes down this road, houses on one side of the road. On this side, on the left side is a set of woods. On the right side is another road behind those houses, and on the other side of that is open fields and pasture.

The paperboy is walking along in the fresh snow. The snow's crunching. The snowplows hadn't really been out yet. He's walking along a side road, freezing, muttering to himself that he hates this job, and he wants to go home. How miserable his life is. And he suddenly hears something in the woods behind the houses crunching and its breaking sticks, and it's making noises, and it starts to draw his attention. And as he goes from house to house, delivering the papers, he notices that whatever is back there is coming along with him, no matter how far down the road he goes, this is coming down the woods with him on behind the houses.

The boy gets to where every time he gets between houses, he's looking back in there. He's trying to see if he can see something, and the longer he goes, the more he is certain that there is someone back there. And of course, this is 1981. It's also not that long after Johnny Gosch and Eugene Wade Martin, paperboys, disappeared. It's fresh on everybody's mind. And he's got a lot of things going on in his head. And he looks over, gets between one set of houses, and he sees what he thinks is an incredibly tall man in a fur coat. And he's looking at this guy, and he's like, it's not a coat, it's a full outfit this guy is wearing. What is this? And he thinks that guy has got to be 8–10 feet tall. This thing is huge.

He's freaked out. Naturally, he goes to the next house. He gets between them, the next two houses, and it's moving closer. Then he realizes that's not a suit. This thing is covered in hair. Terrified, he turns around and runs all the way back home. Of course. He gets back to his house, the dad's standing there. He's got a bag full of papers. "You didn't complete your route." "No, but Dad...." "'But Dad' nothing, you need to go back out and you need to complete that route." "But Dad, you don't understand." "No, out there, complete the route. I don't want to hear anything." He goes back out to complete his route. He's walking down the same road and sees giant footprints in the snow.

The paperboy runs home and gets his dad, and by the time they got back, the plows had come through. No more footprints.

Iowa is crawling with cryptids, and people don't realize it. Corn-fed cryptids there.

Waterloo

As reported in the *Daily Iowan*, the University of Iowa newspaper, an encounter with Bigfoot occurred in 2009 when brothers Seth and Jesse Alne founded the Calhoun County Paranormal Investigators. The Iowa-based ghost hunter group ventured into the woods on a dirt trail on a cool spring evening with their cameras and flashlights.

Eerie sounds were lurking behind trees in the dark shadows of the night. The brothers decided to split up to cover more ground. Jesse avoided going into a flooded area when he saw a hairy creature approaching him. This beast was big, with glowing red eyes. It pushed over a massive tree and glared at him with evil intent.

Jesse yelled out to Seth, saying that he saw Bigfoot. The brother began pursuing the creature, but it ran away, barreling through shrubs and trees. The Sasquatch was too fast, outrunning the brothers into the dark night and deeper into the woods.

The Alne brothers' Calhoun County Paranormal Investigators, an Iowa-based ghost hunter group, researched Bigfoot. The organization made a two-hour documentary that can be seen on YouTube called *Squatch Iowa*. It is well worth watching and has more than 148,000 views.

The Ottosen Sightings of 1978

According to the article "Iowa Bigfoot Sightings" on the website Hangar 1 Publishing, the small north-central town of Ottosen had multiple witnesses and reports from both adults and children of a stocky, nearly five-foot-tall, "hairy, ape-like animal with fangs and deep-set eyes" that lurked in the shadows. Word quickly spread of the creature's sightings, causing a media frenzy. The residents of the town banded together to track down the beast in the nearby woods and cornfields, but it vanished as quickly as it had appeared.

LAKE AND RIVER MONSTERS

Lake Okoboji

Lake Okoboji has depths ranging from 22 feet to more than 140 feet, created by the glaciers from the ice age thousands of years ago. It's the perfect place for a lake monster to live.

Various Algonquin Indian tribes speak of an aquatic dragon commonly known as the "Underwater Panther." It's a cross between a cougar and a dragon that lives in deep water and causes men and women to drown.

The Lake Okoboji Monster, locally called Obojoki, is described as large and dark green/brown in color. It has been known to knock people out of their boats. Some believe it to be some kind of giant fish, while others say it is a sea serpent. *N'west Iowa* called it "the Okoboji version of the Loch Ness Monster."

In 1903, Mr. and Mrs. Charles Barlett reported seeing something splashing in the lake from their boat. The *Vindicator* and *Republican* newspapers reported, "They saw something or rather saw where something was. They have no idea what it was. It might have been a sea serpent, or it might have been some kind of a fish that had grown to an unusual and extraordinary size. They were out on the lake in a boat, when they noticed a short distance from them a terrible commotion in the water. The thing, whatever it was, was moving quite rapidly through the water and quite close to the top and had the appearance of being as large as an overturned skiff." The waves made by Obojoki tipped over the boat.

In 2001, a mother and her two children were staying at a resort overlooking the lake. That day, when they went to the dock, they saw a large, humped body about five feet long with snake-like patterns and said it looked like a cross between a lizard and a horse. The creature took a long breath and headed to the dock, hitting it and shaking the wooden planks.

Keokuk Sea Monster

In April 1913, a seventy-eight-foot sea serpent was swimming around the cofferdam (Lock and Dam No. 19, the junctions of the Des Moines and Mississippi Rivers). The dam workers who saw the creature described it as "covered with scales, a green, slimy leviathan." People who saw the river monster said it was more snakelike than a fish, with a head as big as a bull.

The Lake Okoboji monster, which has been compared to the Loch Ness monster. *Courtesy Bruce Walters.*

A *Daily Gate City* article said, "Imagine the most horrible dragon you can think of and you have Keokuk Sea Monster."

In the summer of 1918, the Keokuk Sea Monster was spotted by three fishermen. In 1919, several people reported seeing the sea serpent swimming around Lake Keokuk. J.B. Worley and James Alexander were swimming south of the old oil station. The creature was described as having "a dog's head and a mouth full of cruel, sharp teeth." Its neck was said to be eighteen inches thick.

While Elmer Beck and his sons, Robert and Hearld, were fishing, the Keokuk Sea Monster swam around their boat.

Big Blue, Mason City

Big Blue is an Iowa cryptid, a monstrous snapping turtle described as being as big as a Volkswagen Beetle and seen by fishers, swimmers and divers. The giant turtle is dangerous. It uses its enormous jaws to try to bite swimmers. Park officials stated that there is no evidence that the monster exists. Locals claim that the legend is real.

The *Metamorphosis* Sculpture

A human-like insect—larger than a man—is frozen in a ten-foot-long stride. Its failing arms are extended—all four of them. It stands not in a summer blockbuster, nor in your nightmares, but on a lawn in west Davenport.

Metamorphosis, by Jacob McGinn, is a metal sculpture recently installed in a neighborhood at the intersection of 4th Street and Telegraph Road, easily viewed from the street. The sculpture's welded-metal surface is perfect for an insect's hard exoskeleton. Its repeated rough forms and forward tilt express a sense of motion.

In spite of its alarming form, its suggested movement—countered by a somewhat symmetrical pose—does not feel predatory or threatening. Although it has bulging eyes and a horned head, the face is surprisingly gentle. It is fascinatingly contradictory work.

In a statement about his work, McGinn wrote, "The piece started as scraps of metal that were welded together. After a while it began to look more insect-like, and I was told to read 'The Metamorphosis' by Franz

Kafka. The story influenced me to create a piece with insect body parts and human-like features." The translated story begins, "One morning Gregor Samsa woke in his bed from uneasy dreams and found he had turned into a large verminous insect."

Samsa's transformed body has an armor-like back. Its many legs wave helplessly before his eyes. The author never explains the character's transformation. There is no indication that the character deserved it.

The sculpture's inexpressive face and gestures convey the same emotional detachment felt in the story. Its rusted surface and the use of discarded materials evoke Kafka's theme of rejection.

Both the story and the artwork are not simple puzzles to solve when missing pieces are found. They reach toward the unfathomable. Questions about perception, reality, normalcy, rationality and judgment are asked but not answered.

The sculpture's placement in a quiet neighborhood makes the artwork more enigmatic. Like Kafka's first sentence, there is a jarring juxtaposition of the mundane and the inexplicable. Art can make the ordinary strange

The *Metamorphosis* sculpture by Jacob McGinn. *Courtesy Bruce Walters.*

and the strange ordinary, and that's true of this sculpture, especially when seen in context with its surroundings.

Metamorphosis was purchased by Tom Chouteau, a Davenport artist best known for his astonishing kaleidoscopes, and installed at his home. Chouteau first saw the sculpture in Dubuque, where it was temporally displayed as part of the city's Art on the River public art program. "I drove by it probably 20 times that day," he said. "It was the most incredibly alive sculpture I've ever seen—nothing abstract about it! It was alive and organic. The feeling I got from the sculpture is that it's comfortable in its skin but nervous about where it has to go next."

Chouteau is planning to install additional sculptures on his property in the near future. "Sculptures," he said, "play off each other so nicely. If you're going to have more than one sculpture, I think it's good to have three."

WHERE: 4 THODE COURT (AT THE INTERSECTION OF 4TH STREET AND TELEGRAPH ROAD), DAVENPORT.

UFOS IN IOWA

Osceola, Sioux City and Davenport, 1878 and 1897

Iowa's connection with mysterious airships began long before they were called flying saucers or UFOs. The earliest recorded sighting in Iowa came on August 7, 1869.

On February 1, 1878, the *Hampton Chronicle* newspaper reported that a young man, crossing the fields in Osceola Township, was attracted by light moving some distance ahead. It stopped and came directly at him with great velocity, stopping abruptly a few feet away. It then rose in the air before descending where he stood. As the light followed him, it was also seen by other witnesses before disappearing.

In 1897, mysterious sightings of an airship were made across the state, beginning in Sioux City on February 3. The airship was described as lingering about eight hundred feet off the ground with a bright light that beamed in the darkness. It then circled in the sky before disappearing into the horizon as quickly as it had appeared.

The airship was spotted above rural farms, small towns and cities. According to the February 3, 1897 *Sioux City Journal*, "The first those people

UFOs in Iowa. *Courtesy Bruce Walters.*

noted was the large white light that would shine from the front of the airship while two smaller lights were seen on the body. The white front light was described as larger than the headlight on a train."

The last reported sighting in Iowa was described in the *Davenport Democrat* on April 13, 1897: "Several hundred people may have witnessed the mysterious flying object over Davenport after 8:00 p.m. the night before. Reporters said it was hard to see as there was a break in a cloud-filled sky as a thunderstorm was approaching. The light from the front of the ship was described as pure white in color that seemed to flare up and glow as it traveled through the sky. It slowly flew away towards the horizon then stopped briefly while the light flared again, then it disappeared into the gathering storm clouds."

Council Bluffs, 1977

The Midwest is jokingly called "Flyover Land." Could this be true for UFOs as well?

On a winter night, something happened in Council Bluffs that was witnessed by multiple people, leaving physical evidence, but it still hasn't been fully explained.

Mike Moore was twenty-four in 1977 when he and his ex-wife drove through Big Lake Park at 7:45 p.m. and spotted something in the night sky. At first, he thought it was an aircraft from nearby Eppley Field in Omaha; however, the longer they watched it, the less plane-like it seemed. "All I seen was this ball coming down," Mr. Moore said. "It was pretty high in the sky." Then suddenly it turned into "a big ball of flame."

Mr. Moore and his wife weren't the only ones to see it. A group of teenagers and then the fire department also watched the mysterious event. Mike Moore's father, Jack, was the assistant fire chief. He responded to the area fifteen minutes later. Jack Moore spotted the point of impact, four by six feet in size, describing it as a "mass of metal." In an interview with the Council Bluffs newspaper the *Daily Nonpareil*, he said, "It was running, boiling down the edge of the levee. The center was too hot to touch."

After the metal cooled down, it was loaded onto the firetruck. "When they left," Mike Moore said, "I kinda hung around and picked up a few pieces. I still have boxes of it in my shed. A grind won't cut it, and you can't even bend it."

Samples of the metal were taken to Griffin Pipe Company and the Ames Laboratory at Iowa State University. It was reported that the debris was smelter slag. The findings didn't convince Mike Moore much. "To take that much molten iron, you'd have to have it at 2000 degrees. There were about 1000 pounds of molten iron laying on the ground."

Other theories tell of a secret military weapon or aircraft that went wrong. Witnessed by eleven people, including firefighters, this sighting is still unexplained.

WHERE: 2600 NORTH 8TH STREET, COUNCIL BLUFFS.

Bedford, 1996

Dean Beamer and his son James were checking on their soybean crop in 1996 when they discovered the crop circles in the middle of their six-hundred-acre field. "Oh, I never did believe in anything like that," Dean said. "But after that, I don't know."

The crop circles puzzled the father and son, as well as residents of the town. Other crop circles have appeared in various areas over the state, including Montour, Marshalltown and near Des Moines, to name a few.

Quad Cities

According to the National UFO Reporting Center, there have been nearly one hundred sightings in the Quad Cities since 2000. *Eerie Quad Cities* includes the stories of a few of them.

THE ST. ELIZABETH PREMONITION

The St. Elizabeth fire is the saddest story in this book. It's a tragedy that still shakes the city of Davenport to the core and has for decades. We decided to let local historian and author Doug Smith talk about the events in his own words:

> *THE HISTORY OF THE HOSPITAL*
> *Despite what the description states below the photo, this was actually a building for insane women, not an insane building.*
>
> *Originally, at Mercy Hospital (now Genesis West) general patients, the mentally ill, and the Sisters were all housed in the same building. After two years of this arrangement, however, it was decided to separate the mentally ill and retarded from the rest of the residents.*

In 1872 a hospital for the Insane was built. This was a four-story structure, built about 100 yards from the original hospital, expressly for the care of the mentally ill, both men and women. This photo shows the front section of the building, with its windows trimmed in decorative white brick corbels. Later they would name it St. Elizabeth's Hospital after Mother Borromeo's baptismal name.

Bridget O'Brien, AKA Sister Mary Aloysia, died on Dec. 18, 1872, of tuberculosis at the age of 21. Hers was the first death in the community of Sisters. She was buried in the Sisters' cemetery located on the grounds, pictured on the far right of this photo.

In 1876, the Sisters of Mercy added a small three-story frame structure close to, but not attached to, the rear of St. Elizabeth's, naming it the "Magdalen Hospital for Wayward Girls." The county had been sending pregnant unwed mothers to St. Elizabeth's for hospitality and other needs for years. These girls had to be housed in St. Elizabeth's for lack of room in the general hospital. Believing there were enough of these women to support additional space, the new structure was built exclusively for them. However, the Sisters underestimated the community's growing needs, and the Magdalen Hospital had a short life. In 1883, St.

ST. ELIZABETH INSANE BUILDING FOR WOMEN, MERCY HOSPITAL—DAVENPORT.

Postcard of St. Elizabeth. *Courtesy Doug Smith.*

Elizabeth's Hospital, which was primarily for women, could no longer accommodate the large number of insane patients coming from all over Iowa and sometimes from Illinois. The solution was to build a separate building for men (St. John's Hospital) and reserve St. Elizabeth's for women. In 1886, the Magdalen Hospital was razed and replaced with a brick addition built onto the rear of St. Elizabeth's (shown here), which could now accommodate about 100 female patients.

In 1930, there were approximately sixty Sisters assigned to the three hospitals—Mercy, St. Elizabeth's, and St. John's. All administrative and management positions were held by Sisters, as were all domestic duties in the convent. Yet the number of Sisters assigned to Davenport began to decline. Thirty-five sisters still controlled all key positions in 1948.

In August of 1949, a remodeled 30-bed unit was dedicated on the first floor of the 1872 St. Elizabeth's building. In this beautifully redesigned unit, qualified professionals under the direction of psychiatrists cared for acute neurological and psychiatric patients, both men and women, using new treatments such as insulin, electric shock, and empirical drugs.

At that time, most of the women living on the upper floors of St. Elizabeth's had been there for many years and would finish out their days receiving "life care." Some of the elderly women had not had a visitor for years. The census for the building as of January 6, 1950, was 63 patients, ranging in age from 20 to 90.

On Friday, January 6th, 1950, the last admission to the new unit arrived at 8 P.M. Later that night, at 2 A.M., Mr. Francis, a night orderly in the general hospital, was suddenly alerted to a bright sky full of flames shooting high above the St. Elizabeth's building and blowing in the high wind across the Mercy Complex. He set off the fire alarm at 2:01 A.M.

The Fire

Bret Grimes wrote *The St. Elizabeth Hospital Fire in Iowa*. He sat for an interview with us and described the events after the fire started at the hospital:

When the fire started, there was, there was some, some feedback from other buildings nearby, particularly the wing of the hospital where obstetrics and gynecology existed. And so, they had seen some type of flashing lights in the middle of the night. And so, you know, a flashing light

The St. Elizabeth Hospital fire in Davenport, January 6, 1950. *Courtesy Bruce Walters.*

kind of stands out. They originally thought that it was an ambulance that was just coming, coming up the driveway. The assumption was an ambulance pulling up there, but it wasn't an ambulance. By that time, Elnora Epperly would have exited the building. There were a few phone calls that went to the fire department, which would have gone down to Central Fire as well as Station Six. Alvin Crandon was at Station Six. That's on Marquette Street. That building still exists. It's an awesome looking building. It's been turned into a house now. And they would have high-tailed it up north and probably got there within about two minutes of that call going out at 2:06 am. The assumption is they got there around 2:08. By the time they get there—it's a lost cause. The building burned fast.

The fire doubled every 30 seconds. They did not have a chance to get much of anybody out. When they get there, it's to a large building, and they quickly find out that there are iron bars in the windows and that they have people that are mentally ill that are inside of it, and so the ability to get people in and out of there would have been rather difficult.

According to information in the Richard-Sloane Special Collections at the Davenport Library, efforts were made to go to the Mercy Hospital Maintenance Room "in hopes of getting a blow torch or saws to use on the bars. That room was locked, and they were unable to gain entrance to the tools."

In the middle of the building, there was a dumbwaiter that ran from the basement to the third floor. Rescuers who attempted to enter the basement reported flames coming out of the dumbwaiter, which prevented them from getting across the room to access the stairs to the upper floor.

Mr. Grimes said there was an eeriness to the events too:

> *They started to usher people out. They were all dressed in either black or white robes and in the dark of the night, it kind of looked like ghosts wandering around the lawn.*
>
> *They had the nurses' convent, which is where the Catholic Sisters that were nurses actually lived. It was right next door to St. Elizabeth and so, so they started to receive people, essentially when they were leaving the building, and they were all dressed in either black or white robes. In the dark of the night, it kind of looked like ghosts wandering around the campus there.*
>
> *The fire department would have helped people over to the main hospital, anybody that was injured that was able to get out. And then slowly you started to have other alarms. I think the second alarm, well actually what they call the third alarm, but it would have been the second in order, came out, around 2:17 am. Pretty quickly they realized that they needed more help. The fire burned for around 90 minutes. It was all done by 3:45 am.*
>
> *At that point, the north wall collapsed. The fire pushed north because there was a southwest wind. Almost everybody that they recovered was from that Southwest corner of the building.*
>
> *There were 107 firefighters involved. And it was, it was everybody. It was Green Acres. Second alarmers down in Fort Bend or ALCOA (they had their fire department and a fire chief). There was also the Rock Island Arsenal fire chief. Everybody that was available came that night. There was one injury documented from the Fire Department. One of the guys got frostbite because it was so cold, and of course, there was a ton of water.*

The Premonition

Forty patients and one nurse perished in the fire. The one nurse was Anna Neal. All the other nurses survived.

Bret Grimes noted, "Anna Neal was 55 years old. She had been married 40 days before the fire. She was a seasoned nurse, a nurse who's been around a while, seemed to know things that people don't know. She met with this, this religious group on Wednesdays at one of the churches. She said that she had a premonition....There's a newspaper article sometime shortly thereafter that mentions it [the *Daily Times*]. She said that she saw a big fire in the near future. She met every Wednesday and so that was four days prior to the fire. That would have been on January 3rd, and the fire happened Friday night into early Saturday morning."

The *Daily Times* newspaper article was titled, "Friends Tell of Mrs. Neal's Prophecies of Tragedy." According to the report, she said that "a great fire which will take between 40–50 lives."

Mr. Grimes laments, "Anna could have survived. She was the one that let Elmer Everly out. But she kept going back in trying to save people. W.F. Schmidt, who worked for the hospital, was the person that remembers her saying that."

Mrs. Neal was found by the firefighters in that patient's room on the upper floor. It appeared that she had gone to help the other patients but lost her own life in the process.

Final Words

The Darker Side of Davenport Walking Tour by the German American Heritage Center summed up the St. Elizabeth fire: "The site of the fire is now the MercyOne Genesis Medical Center, West Central Park, and home to a small cemetery in honor of those that perished. 16 of the victims are buried at that site. St. Elizabeth's fire remains one of the greatest tragedies in Iowa history."

Where: St. Elizabeth has burned down. The cemetery is located on the grounds of MercyOne Genesis Medical Center, Central Park, 1351 West Central Park, Davenport.

MARS HILL CHURCH

Mars Hill Church and the graveyard beside it lie isolated in rural Iowa. One needs to drive for miles on a desolate gravel road before they finally come into view. The one-room church was built of hewn logs between 1850 and 1857. The oldest grave in the cemetery dates back to 1846. Here is the resting place of a Civil War Medal of Honor recipient Sergeant John Donaldson, who captured the Confederate flag at the Appomattox Courthouse hours before Robert E. Lee surrendered.

The church served as a stop on the Underground Railroad, where John Brown is believed to have once hidden slaves. Because there simply isn't a written record to support these claims, applications to the National Park Service's Network to Freedom stations on the Underground Railroad have not been approved. The site, however, was entered into the State of Iowa Register of Historic Places on September 13, 1974, and into the National Register of Historic Places eleven days later.

In the 1980s, a "Satanic panic" seized the nation as some hysterical people became convinced that a vast network of devil-worshippers operated in our midst. Conspiracy theorists alleged that thousands of people a year were being killed by a network of Satanists. One psychiatrist called it "a hidden

The Mars Hill Church is the site of ghosts, UFO sightings and Satanic cults. *Courtesy Bruce Walters.*

holocaust." Investigating police, however, have not been able to substantiate any of the allegations of organized cult abuse in more than twelve thousand documented accusations.

Sadly, vandals defiled the church, scrawling Satanic symbols and crosses in blood on its walls and shattering gravestones in 1985. Two decades later, five teenagers (ages fifteen to nineteen) were arrested for setting a fire that nearly destroyed the church. After two years of construction, the church was rededicated on June 8, 2008.

Mars Hill Church holds a place near the top of Iowa's list of haunted sites. The nearby Cry Baby Bridge and reports of UFO sightings add to its strangeness. Maybe it's simply knowing these stories that lends it an aura of eeriness, but a palpable sense of mystery and unease permeates the air.

As one additional note, Mars Hill is the Roman name for a hill in Athens, Greece, where the god of war, Ares (Mars), stood trial for the murder of Poseidon's son. At least that's the story according to Greek mythology. Its biblical significance is that Paul delivered a sermon at a church of this name.

Where: 1011 100th Avenue, Bloomfield.

Earling Exorcism

Peg Rounds, a paranormal investigator for Whispering Soul Paranormal, said of possessions, "From all my research there has never been a possession. Remember that possessions are very rare even according to the church. Statistics are 1 out of 5,000 cases are a possession, but nowadays everyone is jumping on the bandwagon due to television and TikTok. It's all for getting attention. Most cases are proven to be mental illness."

Despite the incredibly high odds, the Earling Exorcism in 1928 was the real deal, heavily documented in books, articles and documentaries, including a German pamphlet translated in 1935 called *Begone Satan!: A Soul-Stirring Account of Diabolical Possession*. Author William Peter Blatty described reading *Begone Satan!* when researching for his book *The Exorcist* and was inspired to write the novel because of the Earling Exorcism and another case of demonic possession he heard about while attending Georgetown University in 1950. The movie *The Exorcism of Anna Ecklund* also explores this event.

After twenty-eight days of an exorcism ritual at the Convent of the Franciscan Sisters, Emma Schmidt (also referred to as "Anna Ecklund" or

The Earling Exorcism was a twenty-eight-day battle with a demon that inspired both the book and film *The Exorcist*. *Courtesy Bruce Walters.*

"Mary X") was finally freed of the demon that had had terrorized her for twenty-six years.

In 1928, Emma Schmidt was forty-six years old and living in Wisconsin when she began hearing screaming voices like she did in the past. She sought help at the convent in Earling, Iowa, arranged by a Capuchin monk (a member of the Order of Friar Minor Capuchin) from Wisconsin. He performed the first exorcism in June 1912, whose effects, though deemed successful, were also short-lived.

Emma was born in 1882 in Marathon, Wisconsin. Her mother died in 1890, leaving Emma with an abusive and alcoholic father. A devout Catholic at the age of fourteen, she found herself unable to enter a church without suffering from violent thoughts entering her mind.

Emma spoke and understood languages she hadn't been taught. She blasphemed when holy relics were in her vicinity. Emma had the ability to detect and reject food that was blessed. She foamed at the mouth with uncontrolled rage, and her body became distorted.

Dozens of doctors tried to help her but were unsuccessful. The Catholic Church finally set up an exorcism. Father Theophilus Riesinger, a Capuchin monk and experienced exorcist, conducted the exorcism. He was assisted by an old friend, Reverend Joseph Steiger. A dozen nuns were also in attendance. The exorcisms were performed in three different sessions: August 18–26, September 13–20 and December 15–23.

The nuns removed buckets of foul-smelling green vomit and other bodily fluids, although Emma hardly ate. Strange voices and howling animal noises emanated from her body. A pea-sized lump appeared and moved all over her body. Her head became red and so swollen that the nuns feared it was going to explode. Several witnesses saw her levitating to the ceiling. Curious people from miles around lined up outside the brick convent.

Finally, on December 23, after Father Riesinger and the demons wrestled back and forth for several weeks, it was over. At 9:00 p.m., Emma leaped from her bed. The nuns moved to wrestle her back down, but instead she fell back and softly muttered, "Beelzebub, Judas, Jacob, Mina....Hell—hell—hell!"

She suddenly regained consciousness and stated to her stunned audience, "From what a terrible burden have I been freed at last! My Jesus, Mercy! Praised be Jesus Christ!"

By 1935, Father Riesinger had performed nineteen successful exorcisms.

WHERE: CONVENT OF THE FRANCISCAN SISTERS, 207 2ND STREET, EARLING.

The Goddess of West Branch

Along a quiet path in West Branch, Iowa, there is a seated figure cast in bronze. A seven-and-a-half-foot statue of the Egyptian goddess Isis, sculpted by Auguste Puttemans, was gifted by the Belgian people to Herbert Hoover for his humanitarian efforts during World War I. The statue isn't as joyful or celebratory as one might think. It is, unexpectedly, chilling and austere.

Isis, Goddess of Life, by Belgian sculptor Auguste Puttemans. *Courtesy Bruce Walters.*

Originally installed on the Stanford University campus in 1922, the statue was relocated to Iowa at the Herbert Hoover National Historic Site in 1939 according to Spencer Howard's article "Isis, the Wandering Goddess" from the National Archives. "The Hoover family explained that the statue was originally intended to be placed at Herbert Hoover's birthplace, which was actually a polite fiction."

The former president simply didn't like it and had it moved some two thousand miles away.

Isis sits powerfully in stern grandeur on a throne; a lamp with three flames in her left hand symbolizes past, present and future; and an ankh—representing life and life after death—is held in the other. Her face is hidden under a veil.

Plutarch wrote about a sculpture of veiled Isis nearly two thousand years ago. The ancient sculpture was located in a temple in the ancient Egyptian city of Sais. It bore the same inscription as the one in West Branch: "I am all that has been and is and shall be; and no mortal has ever lifted my veil."

A poem written in 1796 by Friedrich Schiller ends after a young man peers under the statue's veil. He is driven mad by his forbidden act. Occultist Madame Blavatsky, in her 1877 book *Isis Unveiled*, asserted that neither science nor philosophy could ever meaningfully pierce the shrouded mystery of the goddess of life.

Note: In West Branch, the sculpture is jarringly out of place between the Presidential Library and the plain, preserved village of Hoover's childhood. Visitors who pass her on the way to Hoover's childhood home may feel an inexplicable eeriness, as if the goddess herself is watching, yet her veiled eyes reveal nothing.

Where: 210 Parkside Drive, West Branch, 52358, on the grounds of the Herbert Hoover National Historic Site.

Mysterious Mounds of Iowa

The Davenport City Cemetery was established in 1843. The graveyard is almost as old as Davenport itself and is older than the state of Iowa. There were three early cemeteries in the area, but the Davenport City Cemetery is the only one existing today. The first plots became available in August 1844. Many of the early records were lost in an office building fire in 1881.

The mysterious mound of Davenport City Cemetery. *Courtesy Bruce Walters.*

Also known as City Cemetery or the Old City Cemetery, it is the site of a mysterious mound located at the northeast corner of the burial grounds. For years, rumors and speculation swirled around like a maelstrom about what was beneath. Was it the final resting place for an elephant that died while performing in a circus in Davenport? Was it the site of a prehistoric Native America burial? Was it a massive grave for those who perished during a cholera epidemic?

As a matter of fact, it's none of the above.

The Elephant Legend

The Richard-Sloane Special Collection at the Davenport Library noted, "The weirdest one, so far, claims that an elephant from a traveling circus died in Davenport and was buried in the mound. In some versions, the elephant went berserk, killed two clowns, and was put down before being buried in the mound."

As strange as that claim sounds, the events surrounding it are true. On July 17, 1972, the Clark and Walters Circus came to Oquawka, Illinois, which is about sixty miles from the Quad Cities. The event was sponsored by the village's Youth Baseball Association. There were going to be two shows that night, at 6:00 p.m. and 8:00 p.m., at the park in the center of the town. Tickets were only one dollar. The star of the show was Norma Jean, a twenty-nine-year-old Asian elephant that weighed 6,500 pounds. It was going to be a fun time for all. Unfortunately, Mother Nature had other plans and interrupted the show with a big storm. The elephant's caretaker, Red Possum, tied her to a tree in the park with a metal chain. Lightning struck the tree, and voltage traveled through the chain, electrifying the elephant and killing her instantly. A dozer had to be brought in to dig a hole big enough to bury her.

But no elephants were buried in the Davenport City Cemetery.

Native American Burial Mounds

"The State of Iowa recognizes the mound as potentially being part of a Native American Burial Mound," as noted in the Richard-Sloane Special Collection at the Davenport Library. But no Native Americans have been laid to rest at the mound either.

Cholera Victims' Burial Site Legend

"Others believe a less sensational tale, that the mound covers cholera victims from an 1873 epidemic," according to the Richard-Sloane Special Collection at the Davenport Library. "Both the monthly reports to City Council and Sexton Kann's personal log do show that there was an epidemic in 1873. Local newspapers also tell of the victims that perished. However, our research can find only 31 people buried at City Cemetery who died of cholera. Other victims of this epidemic were buried in other Davenport cemeteries. All cholera victims buried in the City Cemetery were buried in the Public Ground located in the eastern section of the 'old' cemetery—not the mound area."

To solve the mystery of the mound, geologist Chad Goings of Rolling Hill Consulting Services of Washington, Iowa, did a recent survey using a ground-penetrating radar machine to reveal the secret of what lies beneath.

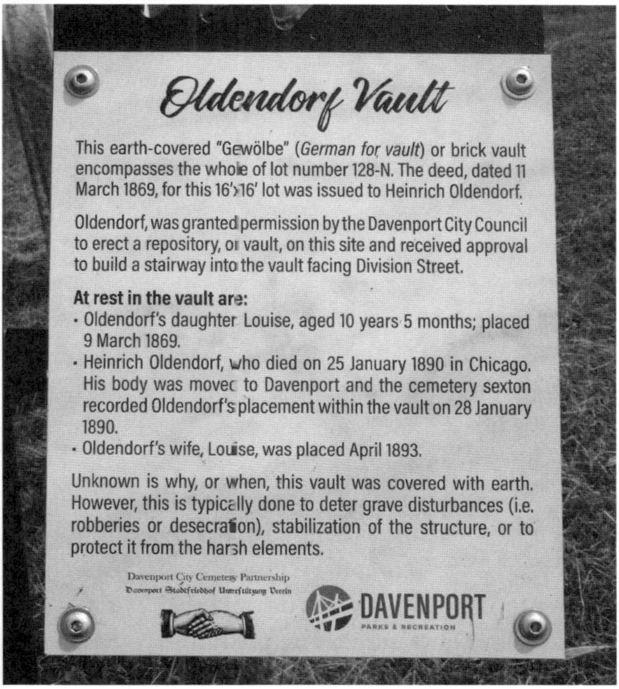

The sign at the Davenport City Cemetery at the mysterious mound. *Courtesy Michael McCarty.*

What he found was an earth-covered vault of three Davenport residents from the 1800s. A plaque in front of the mound explains:

> *This earth-covered "Gewölbe" (German for vault) or brick vault encompasses the whole of lot 128-N. The deed dated March 11, 1969, for this 16' x 16' lot was issued to Heinrich Oldendorf. Mr. Oldendorf was granted permission by the Davenport City Council to erect a repository, or vault, on this site and received approval to build a stairway into the vault facing Division Street.*
>
> *At rest in the vault are: Oldendorf's daughter, Louise, age 10 years and 5 months, placed 9 March 1869. Heinrich Oldendorf, who died on 25 January 1890 in Chicago. His body was moved to Davenport and the cemetery sexton recorded Oldendorf's placement within the vault on 28 January 1890. Oldendorf's wife, Louise, was placed April 1893.*
>
> *Unknown is why, or when this vault was covered with earth. However, this is typically done to deter grave disturbance (i.e., robberies or desecration), provide stabilization of the structure, or to protect it from the harsh elements.*

Although the secret of the mound has been revealed, the mystery of why this happened is unsolved.

WHERE: THE DAVENPORT CITY CEMETERY IS LOCATED OFF WEST RIVER DRIVE, BETWEEN STURDEVANT AND DIVISION STREETS AND ROCKINGHAM ROAD IN DAVENPORT, IOWA.

The Davenport Tablets

In 1874, Reverend Jacob Gass gathered up small relics from ancient earthen mounds on a farm in southeast Davenport, near the Mississippi River. His excavations damaged the mounds irretrievably, destroying graves that had been undisturbed for millennia. Three years later, he unearthed two small slate tablets with mysterious symbols and stick figures scratched into their surface. Their discovery would grow into an international controversy.

Although Gass and his brother found five more tablets that were immediately dismissed as fakes (and have since disappeared), his discoveries reinforced the belief that the builders originated in Europe or were from the Lost Tribes of Israel. Or they could have been from a "once powerful race, which was exterminated, or has disappeared, to make room for the existing savage tribes"—these words were spoken by Andrew Jackson in his 1830 State of the Union speech.

Thomas Jefferson excavated similar earthen mounds around the time of the American Revolution, giving careful attention to stratification and the position of artifacts. He did not remove these artifacts or any human remains. His conclusion that Native Americans built the mounds is the consensus of scholars and archaeologists today.

Although the Davenport Tablets have been largely dismissed as forgeries, popular books on the ancient past such as Erich von Däniken's 1968 work, *Chariots of the Gods: Unsolved Mysteries of the Past*, brought renewed interest in the tablets. *America BC: Ancient Settlers in the New World* by Barry Fell (1976) contended that Egyptians traveled to Davenport and built the mounds in 800 BC.

Graham Hancock, author of 1995's *Fingerprints of the Gods*, proposed that mound-builders inherited knowledge from an advanced society that existed during the last ice age before a global cataclysm that occurred some twelve thousand years ago. In the case of the Davenport Tablets, Hancock suggested that they could be evidence of prehistoric seafaring civilizations.

This page: Davenport Tablets at the Putnam Museum and Science Center. *Courtesy Putnam.*

2040 West River Drive, Davenport. *Courtesy Bruce Walters.*

Current site of the Davenport Tablets. *Courtesy Bruce Walters.*

Whether the tablets are fakes or genuine, they continue to inspire questions about the origins of civilization.

The earthen mounds no longer exist at the location where Reverend Glass's excavations were made 150 years ago. The present location, 2040 West River Drive, is now the site of chemical warehouses and loading docks.

Knowing that this industrial landscape, tucked behind surveilled fences and gates, is the same site as the ancient burial earthen mounds is almost impossible to reconcile.

Where: 2040 West River Drive, Davenport.

Effigy Mounds National Monument

The Effigy Mounds National Monument in Northeast Iowa protects more than two hundred of these sacred ancient Native American mounds. "Eastern Woodland Indians built mounds from about 500 B.C. until the early European contact period. Prehistoric mounds are common from the plains of the Midwest to the Atlantic seaboard, but only in this region of the Upper Midwest was there a culture that regularly constructed effigy mounds in the shape of mammals, birds or reptiles.

Where: Effigy Mounds National Monument, 151 Highway 76, Harpers Ferry.

Count Nicholas Fejervary

One of the people who shaped Davenport was a Hungarian nobleman. What were the odds?

Count Nicholas Fejervary (Miklós Fejérváry) came to Davenport when he was forty-one years old. He left his native Hungary to escape the imposed martial law that followed the failed revolutions that swept Europe in 1847 and 1848. Friends had been exiled, imprisoned, even executed. He chose to settle in Davenport because it reminded him of his home on the Danube.

It is rumored that he carried a "gripsack full of gold" with him when he arrived. Whether or not this is true, his wealth would increase substantially from the investments he made in land and downtown Davenport real estate.

Octave Thanet, the renowned Davenport author, wrote, "Fejervary was of tall stature, with heavy hair, beard, and eyebrows; handsome, amiable and of particularly obliging manners. Few men enjoy such popularity, respect, and affection as fell to the share of Fejervary who even in his youth was one of the

Portrait of Count Nicholas Fejevary. *Courtesy Bruce Walters.*

most distinguished men of Hont [a historic county of the kingdom of Hungary]. This was due to his firm and stainless character, his mature judgment, his kindness of heart, and the ripe culture of his mind."

During the Civil War, Fejervary was an ardent supporter of the Union. When efforts to erect a monument to Lincoln after his assassination flagged, Fejervary offered to donate twice the amount raised if the monument would be erected to Scott County's Civil War dead instead. After his offer, donations for a monument fund increased. Thanet also wrote, "To him more than to any other citizen do we owe the stately column that tells the world the gratitude of Scott County to its citizen soldiery. He not only gave largely in money, he gave his time and his influence."

The monument stands in the center of the 1100 block of Main Street near Central High School more than 140 years after its dedication on July 4, 1881. Atop the monument column, a Union infantry soldier—a common man—stands in readiness with a rifle.

Among his other acts of charity, he established a Home for Old Farmers of Scott County. The home became a nursing home in the 1960s. The home, at 800 East Rusholme Street, is now the Fejervary Healthcare Center. The trust he established was recently transferred to Iowa State University to create perpetual funding for students pursuing degrees in agriculture. It is estimated that the trust will provide twenty $3,000 scholarships annually.

Fejervary Park is probably his most widely known legacy. Here, he had personally supervised the building of a spacious home, built shortly after his arrival. The brick used to build the house came from clay found on the site.

Nicholas Fejervary died in 1895 at the age of eighty-four. He is buried with his wife, Karoline (1810–1880), and son, Nicholas (1847–1863), at Oakdale Memorial Gardens, section 7, lot 13. His and his wife's gravestone stands, but the smaller stone that marked the grave of their son was crushed in the 2020 derecho. Nicholas never relinquished his lands in Hungary, and his daughter, Celestine, returned to live there.

In her memoriam to Fejervary, Octave Thanet concluded, "He was so quiet in his benefactions that no one, even his daughter probably knows their extent; but the long train of the poor that stood on the streets to watch his last earthly journey, the plainly dressed men and women that came to his home and begged for a last look of their friend—these bore witness."

Fejervary Park

One of Count Nicholas Fejervary's largest legacies to the city of Davenport is the park named after him. In 1902, his surviving daughter, Celestine (1847–1937), gave the seventy-five-acre estate to the city. Three years later, on September 17, 1905, Fejervary Park was opened to the public.

Local historian Doug Smith, author of *Davenport (Postcard History: Iowa)*, described the park's debut in the city:

> *The Grand Opening of Fejervary Park was held on Sunday, September 17, 1905. Professor Otto's Band furnished a concert for the affair from 2 to 5 o'clock. The Tri-City Street Railway Company provided cars for the public on the Fejervary Park branch of its Northwest Davenport line. An immense crowd turned out for the affair, and everyone heartily endorsed the work of the park commissioners, which had made Miss Fejervary's gift into such a fine addition to the city parks. A more favorable day could not have been chosen and hundreds of citizens took advantage of the opportunity. A program of popular music was rendered which the crowd that lined the terraces and walks surrounding the pavilion enjoyed immensely. The rooms were decorated with a profusion of palms, potted plants, and the flower beds and shrubbery on the grounds gave the place an almost tropical appearance. Several new drives and walks had been built as well, making the pavilion more easily accessible.*
>
> *Before the opening of Fejervary Park, the original Fejervary home was completely remodeled, enlarged, and made into an Inn. New chimneys were put on, brick walls were repaired and repainted and the exterior was repainted. The entire building was wired for electricity and steam heated, making it usable in winter as well as summer.*

In 1909, a municipal zoo was added named Mother Goose Land. Among the animals were five buffalo, three elk, two reindeer, two burros, two eagles, four foxes and eight Angora goats, according to an article in the *Quad-City*

Fejervary's tombstone restored at Oakdale Memorial Gardens. *Courtesy Bruce Walters.*

Count Nicholas Fejervary's tombstone after the derecho. *Courtesy Bruce Walters.*

Times. In 1928, Monkey Island opened with seventy rhesus monkeys. It became a major attraction in the Quad Cities.

Over the years, they had a petting zoo, donkey rides, panning for fake gold, a cemetery volcano and Old West village, including a boot hill graveyard for the delight of kids and adults. On a personal note, the McCarty family donated two adult rabbits to the zoo.

In 2009, Mother Goose Land and Monkey Island closed.

Fejervary Park is located on top of a bluff that has a grand view of Davenport with its rolling green hills. Mother Goose Land became the Fejervary Learning Center. There still is a playground and an aquatic center.

Where: Count Nicholas Fejervary is buried at Oakdale Memorial Gardens, 2501 Eastern Avenue, Davenport. Fejervary Park is at 1800 West 12th Street, Davenport.

ABANDONED IN IOWA

Ghost Towns

BUCKHORN

There are ten ghost towns in the state of Iowa. Ghost towns aren't necessarily scary places, despite the name. They are abandoned villages where people once lived and no longer do, either because of an economic collapse or a natural or human-caused disaster. About forty-five minutes north of Maquoketa is Buckhorn, in Jackson County.

Eerie Quad Cities described the town as being "a farming co-op. Not much is left to Buckhorn: a well-maintained cemetery, a creamery building, and a long-ago abandoned church. One of the buildings has graffiti that says, 'Satan's Playground,' which makes the place seem like it is straight out of a horror movie."

BUCKHORN'S HISTORY

The founder of Buckhorn was Shadrack Burleson of New York. He established a claim that became the town of Buckhorn. Mr. Burleson shot deer and nailed their antlers by the door of the inn he built there. The inn was named Buckhorn, and so was the school and the creamery. A settlement eventually sprang up in the area.

Hans Skott and nineteen area farmers obtained loans from the Maquoketa bank and formed Farmer's Union Cooperative Creamery. The coop paid $31,000 to construct the building and buy equipment.

In the 1900s, the average dairy herd was fifteen cows. About 30,000 pounds of butter was produced within the first seven months and increased over the years. Close to 34 million pounds of butter were manufactured from 1899 to 1952, according to an article in the *Maquoketa Sentinel-Press* written by Kelly Gerlach, which quoted sources from interviews with the Skott family and the book *History of the Farmer's Union Co-operative Creamery Company 1899–1963* by R.A. Werden. (Author's note: We wanted a little more information about this book. After searching the Library of Congress, OCLC WorldCat, Secretary of State Illinois Libraries and the University of Iowa library, we came up empty-handed. We wrote to Gerlach to see if she had any additional information about the book, and she said, "I must admit that after more than 5 years, I don't recall the exact source that was referenced. However, R.A. Werden's book may be a small one that was

Original University of Iowa art building (built in 1936), unused since the 2008 flood. *Courtesy Bruce Walters.*

The abandoned church at Buckhorn. *Courtesy Bruce Walters.*

The abandoned creamery at Buckhorn. *Courtesy Bruce Walters.*

printed here in Jackson County for local use. I might have obtained the use of it from the Skott family or our local historical society. I admit, my mind is a little hazy on that subject after all this time, so I don't want to steer you down the wrong path.")

By the late 1950s and early 1960s, the creamery had started to decline, mostly because small dairy operations were selling their businesses to the bigger ones. The one-room school began consolidating into other school districts and merging. Buckhorn Creamery started to produce cheese instead, but that ultimately failed too. In April 1963, the building and acreage were sold in auction.

Bruce Walters went to Buckhorn to take photographs for this book. He said that the church looked like a country church you might see on the side of the road, but the creamery made his skin crawl because it was so empty and unsettling.

Buckhorn has a *Twilight Zone* atmosphere. The first episode of the television series, called "Where Is Everybody," was penned by Rod Serling. It begins as a man walks down a dirt road alone. Everywhere he goes in town, there are signs of life, but nobody is around—the place is empty, a feeling of desertion and isolation around every corner. That same feeling is what makes Buckhorn so eerie. It was once a town where people lived and breathed. Now there is nothing. Could my town be next? Alone and abandoned?

WHERE: 125TH AVENUE, BUCKHORN.

HURSTVILLE

Less than ten miles away from Buckhorn is Hurstville, another ghost town. Four kilns remain. They heated limestone rocks mined from nearby quarries. The process formed lime mortar used in the construction of homes, farm buildings and public buildings throughout the Midwest.

Alfred Hursts built the first kiln in 1871, and three others followed. The operation grew to three thousand acres and fifty employees. He organized the Maquoketa and Hurstville Railroad in 1888 to ship the burned lime instead of hauling it by wagon.

An abandoned building at Hurstville. *Courtesy Bruce Walters.*

Kiln at Hurstville. *Courtesy Bruce Walters.*

By the 1920s, Portland Cement had affected the lime industry. The kilns were shut down in 1930, when William Hurst, Alfred's brother, died. The kilns were restored by the Jackson County Historical Society in 1980.

WHERE: 7301 HURSTVILLE ROAD, MAQUOKETA.

Houses and Buildings

ROSEANNE'S ABANDONED MANSION IN IOWA (ELDON)

Roseanne Barr was born in Salt Lake City, Utah, and eventually became a big name in comedy. By the mid-1980s, things were started to heat up for her. In 1986, she appeared in a Rodney Dangerfield TV special and had a spot on *Late Night with David Letterman*. The year 1987 saw the release of her own HBO special, *The Roseanne Barr Show*, which won "Funniest Female Performance in a TV Special" by the American Comedy Awards. Her "domestic goddess" became a popular catchphrase, and she was offered the role of Peg Bundy in *Married...with Children* but turned it down. Instead, she starred in her own sitcom, *Roseanne*.

Tom Arnold was born in Ottumwa, Iowa. He won first place in the Minneapolis Comedy Competition in the late 1980s and moved out to Los Angeles, where he eventually got hired to write for *Roseanne*. He also appeared regularly as Arnie Thomas.

The *Roseanne* sitcom soared in Nielsen's rating. The series about a working-class American family struck a chord with its viewers, and in 1989–90 it even reached no. 1 and remained in the Top 4 for six of the nine seasons it aired.

Roseanne married Tom Arnold on January 20, 1990. Besides doing the TV series together, they opened Roseanne and Tom's Big Food Diner in Eldon, Iowa (the same town that houses the "American Gothic" house by Grant Wood), in 1993. It had twenty-six employees, making it the biggest employer in the town.

While their four years of marriage were rocky at best, with plenty of negative publicity in the headlines and tabloids, the more interesting aspects of their union involved singing and tattoos. Musically, the couple were a mixed bag. In 1990, Roseanne sang "The Star-Spangled Banner" at a San Diego Padres game. She spat and grabbed her crotch, making fun of baseball players. President George H. Bush called her performance "disgraceful."

On April 1993, Roseanne, Tom Arnold and their band performed at Farm Aid in Ames, Iowa. Cindy and Michael McCarty, who were working for *Oil: The Music Tabloid* at the time, saw the performance. Mr. McCarty commented, "Cindy and I saw Farm Aid in the Press Box and out in the stadium. It was raining during some of the performances, so we'd go to the Press Box, plus they had a great spread. We were seated next to the reporter from the *Des Moines Register*. Their set list included 'Ballad of John & Yoko' (by The Beatles), 'Johnny B. Goode' (by Chuck Berry), 'The Theme from Green Acres' and 'Whole Lotta Shakin' Going On' (by Jerry Lee Lewis). I think everyone expected the worst when the Arnolds hit the stage, but they were quite good, the band was talented, and the couple singing was good enough and they were having a lot of fun doing it."

Tom and Roseanne both got tattoos of each other's names on their bodies. Hers said "Property of Tom Arnold" and was on her right thigh. His tattoo said "Rosie" and was on his behind. Tom had a tattoo portrait of Roseanne's face on the left side of his chest. He got it back in 1994 in a last-ditch effort to save his marriage. After the divorce, the comedian had to suffer through a year and a half of painful laser treatment to get rid of the ink.

In 1994, Roseanne and Tom got divorced, and in February 1995, Roseanne and Tom's Big Food Diner closed. Before that, Tom Arnold and Roseanne were going to build a $16 million, twenty-eight-thousand-square-foot mansion, making it the largest single-family house in the Hawkeye State.

This Victorian-style mansion was located on 1,700 acres of land just outside of Eldon, off the beaten path from where their Big Food Diner was located. In the middle of a cornfield and woods with a lake near their home, the luxury house was going to have a four-lane bowling alley, an indoor swimming pool and a screening room to watch their favorite films. The location would have been ideal for four-wheelers and riding horses.

However, everything came to a halt when the couple separated. They donated the mansion to the Indian Hills Community Foundation, which later sold it to a private company. According to a real estate management company interviewed by the *Des Moines Register* in 2018, the project was too expensive to tear down, leaving an unbuilt luxury mansion decaying in the woods, with crumbling walls, exposed wires and skeletal frames of wooden beams. This potential ritzy getaway is now disintegrating and decaying, desolated and isolated, with an unfinished and haunting vibe to it.

WHERE: THE ROSEANNE AND TOM ARNOLD ABANDONED MANSION IS ON THE OUTSKIRTS OF ELDON, IOWA. THE PLACE IS PRIVATE PROPERTY AND, AS SUCH, SHOULD BE RESPECTED.

DUBUQUE BREWING AND MALTING COMPANY

Construction on the Dubuque Brewing and Malting Company began in 1895 with a $500,000 budget. This was going to be a modern brewery, a state-of-the-art facility of more than 225,000 square feet, with red bricks and Romanesque towers. May 7, 1896, was set for the grand opening.

In its ads, the company boasted making 300,000 barrels of beer annually, although it was more likely around 190,000. The refrigeration plant was said to make more than two hundred tons of ice daily.

Prohibition stopped production for the beer company. It briefly reopened after Prohibition ended. In 1934, the Corn Belt Company turned the place into a meatpacking plant. By the end of World War II, it remained a ham storage facility until it closed in 1949.

In 1977, it was added to the National Register of Historical Places. The movie *F.I.S.T.*—a drama starring Sylvester Stallone, Rod Steiger and Peter Boyle—was shot at the location. *Take This Job and Shove It* was filmed at the brewery. The comedy starred Robert Hays, Barbara Hershey and Art Carney.

Dubuque Brewing and Malting Company. *Courtesy Bruce Walters.*

In 2005, the City of Dubuque protected the property from being demolished. In July 2016, heavy rain caused part of the building's roof to collapse.

In 2024, Dubuque Brewing and Malting Company partially demolished some of the buildings. The future of the place is uncertain.

Note: Photographer Bruce Walters took a photo of the brewery and added some artwork for the cover of Michael McCarty and Terrie Leigh Relf's *Waiting for the Night*, a horror and science fiction short story collection.

Where: 3000 Jackson Street, Dubuque.

Whatever Happened to Black Hawk's Remains?

The Black Hawk's Plaster Cast

An eerie plaster cast of the Sauk warrior and leader Black Hawk is in the Hauberg Museum's collection at the Black Hawk Historic Site in Rock Island, Illinois. According to museum collection records, "It was made as

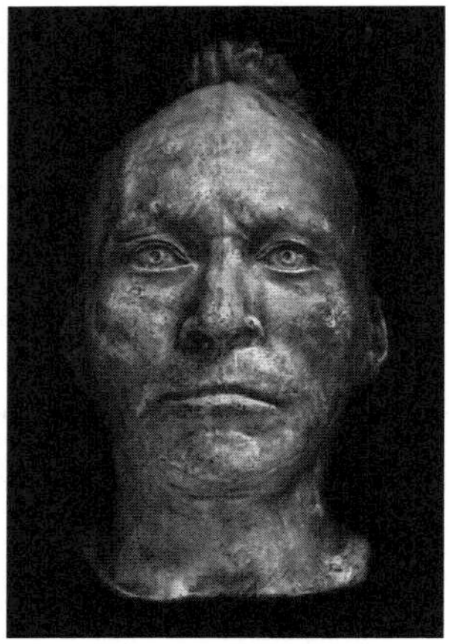

Phrenological bust of Black Hawk from 1838 at the Hauberg Museum. *Courtesy Bruce Walters.*

a phrenological study by the Fowler Brothers." In 1837, the Fowler Brothers' office was in Washington.

The plaster cast hauntingly captured the warrior's exact likeness when he was seventy years old, freezing a singular moment nearly two hundred years ago. Yet it has no sense of warmth. The eyes in life masks are—by necessity—closed or covered and have an introspective quality. However, the eyes of this cast are open. Apparently, they were done after the cast was made. The effect is unnerving.

Phrenology was a pseudoscience that claimed that a person's character and intelligence could be determined by the shape and size of their skull. Its influence peaked in the mid-nineteenth century. As phrenology was often used to confirm racial biases, this bust was of considerable scientific interest when it was made. It now serves as a symbol of Native American resilience and a critique of flawed science. We know Black Hawk in part through this cast, painted portraits and his autobiography, the first told from the perspective of an Indigenous American.

Black Hawk's Life and Legacy

Black Hawk is a familiar name in the Quad Cities. Many of the local banks, roads, businesses, parks, hotels, creeks, schools, a community college, bowling alleys, crematories and even an Iowa county proudly bear the name. The Chicago Blackhawks are named after him, as were four U.S. Navy ships, including a destroyer. Iowa's nickname, the Hawkeye State, is also likely in his honor. The University of Iowa logo is the profile of a black hawk.

This legendary Sauk leader is synonymous with the resistance against westward expansion and its effects on Native American people and their ancestral lands. He is best known for leading the conflict known as the Black Hawk War of 1832, a tragedy that ended with the forced removal of Native American tribes from their land and homes in Illinois. Yet Black Hawk's story did not end with his defeat and surrender in this war. The circumstances surrounding his death, burial and subsequent theft of his remains tell a troubling tale that reflects the broader injustices and indignities suffered by Native Americans.

This section will examine the details of Black Hawk's death, what happened to his body after his passing and the historical and cultural significance of these events. By examining these aspects, we gain insight into the ongoing struggles of Native Americans.

Black Hawk was not a chief. He assumed leadership of a band, not the entire tribe of the Sauk, because of his ferocity in battle. He was born Ma-ka-tai-me-she-kia-kiak in 1767 in the village of Saukenuk on the Rock River (in present-day Illinois). He grew up during a time of increasing pressure on Native American lands by European settlers and the U.S. government.

From an early age, he learned to be a warrior. He made his first kill as a boy. It would not be his last. Nick Vulch in *Early Days in Davenport and Rock Island* noted, "He spent nearly ten pages in his autobiography recounting a host of early kills." Black Hawk's autobiography (translated by Antoine LeClaire), titled *Life of Ma-ka-tai-me-she-kia-kiak* (or *Life of Black Hawk*), was published in 1833.

In 1804, four Sauks and one Meskwaki signed a treaty with the United States, ceding to the government more than 50 million acres of land.

Black Hawk statue at the Black Hawk State Historic Site in Rock Island. *Courtesy Michael McCarty.*

The cession encompassed all Sauk and Meskwaki tribal lands in Illinois, southwestern Wisconsin and northeastern Missouri. The payment received in exchange was $2,234.50 in goods at the time of signing and a $1,000 annuity to be paid ($600 to the Sauks, $400 to Meskwakis). However, the Treaty of 1804 was clearly fraudulent. The five men of the tribes, on their own, had no authority to cede tribal lands to anyone.

Black Hawk was furious when he heard about this. How dare the U.S. government do such a thing? He contended that the tribesmen who signed the treaty didn't have the authority to sign a document on behalf of the tribes. Still, the American government proclaimed the treaty to be valid and legally binding.

In his autobiography, Black Hawk recalled:

> *Quashquame, Pashepaho, Ouchequaka, and Hashequarhiqua were sent by the Sacs to St. Louis to try and free a prisoner who had killed an American. The Sac tradition was to see if the Americans would release their friend. They were willing to pay for the person killed, thus covering the blood debt and satisfying the relations of the murdered man.*
>
> *Upon return, Quashquame and the others came up and gave us the following account of their mission:*
>
> *On our arrival at St. Louis, we met our American father and explained to him our business, urging the release of our friend. The American chief told us he wanted land. We agreed to give him some on the west side of the Mississippi, likewise more on the Illinois side opposite Jefferson. When the business was all arranged, we expected to have our friend released to come home with us. About the time we were ready to start, our brother was let out of prison. He started and ran a short distance when he was SHOT DEAD!*
>
> *This was all they could remember of what had been said and done. It subsequently appeared that they had been drunk the greater part of the time while at St. Louis.*
>
> *This was all myself and our nation knew of the treaty of 1804. It has since been explained to me. I found by that treaty, that all of the country east of the Mississippi, and south of Jefferson was ceded to the United States for one thousand dollars a year. I will leave it to the people of the United States to say whether our nation was properly represented in this treaty? Or whether he received a fair compensation for the extent of the country ceded by these four individuals?*

This did not sit well with Black Hawk. This was his home, and who were they to take it from him and his tribesman? When the War of 1812 reached the area, Black Hawk immediately sided with the British forces against the Americans. Known as the British Band, these warriors twice defeated the Americans, first at the Battle of Campbell's Island in July 1814 and then again at the Battle of Credit Island in September of the same year. Although the British were ultimately defeated, Black Hawk maintained his political allegiance with them for nearly the rest of his life.

Black Hawk fought on the side of the British, but the way they went to battle disturbed him. "Instead of stealing upon each other and taking every advantage to kill the enemy and save their own people, they march out in open daylight and fight. Regardless of the number of warriors, they may lose."

Eventually, the Sauks complained to Thomas Forsyth, the Indian agent in charge of the Sauks and Meskwakis. To their immense surprise, he informed them that by signing the Treaty of 1804, they had officially and legally agreed to give up all their lands to the U.S. government. With the home they had known their entire lives now forfeit, they were ordered to leave the area and relocate to the other side of the Mississippi River to what is now Iowa.

In 1816, Black Hawk's Treaty of Peace ended the hostilities with Americans, the War of 1812, and confirmed the Treaty of 1804. This time, Black Hawk fixed his own mark (signature) on the document. Still, he was apprehensive about signing, and with good reason. According to the treaty, the Sauks were to cede their lands when told to do so by the American government. In later years, Black Hawk said that he had no idea what the treaty was going to do.

That same year, some of the very first white settlers moved into the region when an American fort was constructed on one of the big islands in the Mississippi River. The American surveyors dubbed it Rock Island, and the fort was named Fort Armstrong. The Sauks and the new army residents got along well, especially with the camp settler, a British expatriate, George Davenport. Later, they would get along equally well with the government interpreter assigned to Fort Armstrong, Antoine LeClaire.

While the relationship between the soldiers at the fort and the Sauks was peaceful, the Sauks were still a little sad to see the island occupied. In his autobiography, Black Hawk said, "This [island] was the best one on the Mississippi and had long been the resort of our young people during the summer. It was our garden, like the white people have near their big villages, which supplied us with strawberries, blackberries, gooseberries, plums, apples, and nuts of different kinds. Being situated at the foot of the rapids,

Fort Armstrong re-creation at the Rock Island Arsenal. *Courtesy Bruce Walters.*

its water supplied us with the finest fish. In my early life, I spent many happy days on the island."

Black Hawk and some cf his followers decided to stay. This was their home, and he had no intention of leaving. However, in 1831, they were driven out of Saukenuk by American troops.

The Black Hawk War

In 1832, Black Hawk and more than one thousand of his followers traveled to Prophetstown, Illinois, to plant corn. The group clashed with the American government over the next few months in a conflict that came to be known as the Black Hawk War.

However, the revolt was a short-lived massacre, ending horribly at the Battle of Bad Axe, where several hundred of Black Hawk's followers were slaughtered. Six weeks later, "He was taken prisoner, his two sons, the Winnebago Prophet and five other principal members of the tribe," Vulch wrote in his book.

After several months in prison, Black Hawk toured the East Coast, where he was greeted by large crowds in Washington, Philadelphia and Baltimore. Shortly after his release from captivity, he returned to Iowa, where he asked his friend Antoine LeClaire to translate his life story into English so the people of the United States "might know the cause that had impelled him to acts as he had done, and the principles by which he was governed." This story, written by J.B. Patterson from LeClaire's notes, became the autobiography of Ma-ka-tai-me-she-kia-kiak, becoming the first life story told from the perspective of an American Indian when it was published in 1833. When he returned to Washington in 1837 as part of an Indian delegation, the phrenology study of his head was cast.

Black Hawk's Death and the Theft of His Body

On October 3, 1838, Black Hawk died at the age of seventy-one after suffering from an illness, possibly malaria. His death came the year after the phrenology bust was cast, four years after the publication of his autobiography and five years after his defeat in the Black Hawk War.

Black Hawk was temporarily buried in Agency, Iowa, at the Indian Agency. His remains were soon moved to the Iowaville Cemetery and buried in a stone cairn overlooking the valley below. He wore a U.S. military uniform given to him by Andrew Jackson. Medals given to him by the British, French and American governments were placed on his breast. His old warrior club was placed in front of the tomb.

In the spring of 1839, less than a year after Black Hawk's death, his grave was desecrated and his head stolen by Dr. James Turner, a local settler and dentist. Turner, reportedly motivated by a desire to display Black Hawk's

Top: Gravemarker of Black Hawk at Iowaville Cemetery. However, he was not a chief. *Courtesy Bruce Walters.*

Bottom: Black Hawk grave at the Iowaville Cemetery. Black Hawk's head was stolen from this grave site. *Courtesy Bruce Walters.*

skeleton as a trophy or for sale as a curiosity or for phrenological study, returned later to take the rest of the body. His widow visited the site later and found, to her horror, that the grave had been violated and his body was gone.

Sarah Welsh Nossaman was taking care of Dr. Turner's sister-in-law when he came home at 4:00 a.m., having just stolen Black Hawk's head from his grave. She was thirteen years old. The account of that night and the subsequent days that she recounted when she was much older is ghastly and chilling:

> *In 1837 or 1838, I don't remember which, Black Hawk died of malaria fever. One of our neighbors, Dr. James Turner, thought if he could only steal Black Hawk's head he could make a fortune out of it by taking it east and putting it on exhibition. After two weeks' watching he succeeded in getting it. Black Hawk's burial place was near old Iowaville, on the north side of the Des Moines River, under a big sugar tree. It was there Dr. Turner severed the head from the body. At the time it was done I was taking care of his sick sister-in-law, Mrs. William Turner. The doctor made his home with his brother. We knew the evening he went to steal the head and sat up to await his coming. He got in with it at four o'clock in the morning and hid it till the afternoon of the same day, when he cooked the flesh off the skull. So I can say that I am the only one now living that witnessed that sight, for it was surely a sight for me. If the rest of Black Hawk's bones were ever removed it was a good many years after his head was stolen.*
>
> *The second morning after their ruler's head was stolen ten of the best Indian warriors came to William Turner's and asked for his brother, the Doctor. They were painted war style. He told them he did not know where his brother was. They told him they would give him ten days to find his brother, and if he did not find him in that time he would pay the penalty for his brother's crime. But he knew where his brother was. He was at the home of a neighbor named Robb, Uncle Tommy Robb as he was called by everyone, on the south side of the Des Moines River. But he did not want to find his brother and sent a boy to tell him to fly for Missouri, which he did. The Indians returned to Iowaville to hold council and conclude what to do, and while they were holding council William Turner and his wife made their escape in a canoe down the river. William Turner kept a little store in New Lexington. He got his neighbors to pack and send his goods after him.*

> *But the Indians demanded their ruler's head, and for three weeks we expected an outbreak every day, but through the influence of their agent and the citizens together they gave up hostilities for a time. The whites told them they would bring Turner to justice if he could be found. The sheriff chased Turner around for a while, which only gave him the more time to get out of the way. The Turner family finally all went to St. Louis where the Doctor was found again, and to keep the Indians quiet the sheriff went to St. Louis in search of him, but he did not find him. He did not want to find him. But Turner got frightened and took Black Hawk's skull to Quincy, Illinois, and put it in the care of a doctor there for safe-keeping (I forget the doctor's name) till the Indians would get settled down, and then he intended to take it east. But when he got ready to go east with it the doctor in Quincy refused to give it up, and he did not dare to go to law about it, so after all his trouble and excitement he lost Black Hawk's skull, and not only made Turners endless trouble, but put the lives of all settlers in jeopardy for months.*

The Fate of Black Hawk's Remains

A band of about fifty braves came to Burlington and made a formal complaint to Governor Lucas of Iowa Territory about the desecration. In December 1840, the bones were recovered, brought to Burlington and placed in a box in his office. Singing Bird, Black Hawk's widow, identified the remains and left them in the governor's care. His remains were transferred to Dr. Enos Lowe so they could be given to the soon-to-be-organized Burlington Geological and Historical Society. Tragically, the museum was destroyed in a fire on the night of January 16, 1853—supposedly taking Black Hawk's remains with it.

In yet another twist, recent research by Burlington historian Russ Fry led him to conclude that Black Hawk's remains were not destroyed in the fire. One intriguing clue was found in the minutes of the University of Iowa's Board of Trustees meeting that took place three days after the fire. In the meeting, the former governor submitted a proposal that was accepted and authorized by the board's president for receiving Black Hawk's bones for preservation by the university. However, Lucas died within three weeks of his proposal, and there are no university records of Black Hawk's remains.

Fry, however, discovered newspaper articles and statements made shortly after the fire that indicated that Black Hawk's remains were not destroyed. Fry contends that the box containing the remains was moved to Burlington's

Burlington's potter's field at Greenwood Cemetery, where it is believed Black Hawk was buried. *Courtesy Bruce Walters.*

First Presbyterian Church four years after the fire and were found in 1880 when the church was being torn down. As he wrote, a man was deputized to "consign the bones to a grave at Aspen Grove. The man buried them in the potter's field and left the grave unmarked." A potter's field is where the poor were buried, often by family members but sometimes by the city.

Aspen Grove is a beautiful cemetery that was established in 1843. Just inside the cemetery's south arched entrance is a potter's field—an expansive field of grass with a few trees and stone markers. Any wooden markers are long gone. A lack of detailed records is not uncommon for burials in a potter's field. Interestingly, Russ Fry stated that an "oral history shared among Aspen Grove workers asserts that Black Hawk was buried in a grave marked only by a stick in the potter's field....When I visited Aspen Grove Cemetery, I spoke with the staff in the cemetery office. I asked if Black Hawk is buried here. One staff member confidently replied yes. A moment later, she looked up at me and, carefully amending her initial response, said maybe."

Part II
GHOSTS

Asking if ghosts are real is akin to asking if anxiety is real or if a sense of wonder is real. If we are touched by an experience, then it is "real" in that it has impacted us. When I was young, I was playing in the front of our house when an old man, walking past, paused to look toward me. We held each other's gaze for a moment before he smiled wistfully and continued his walk. I still recall feeling that he was me, nearing the end of my life. Was it simply my imagination, a reflection of something I had overheard of a ghost? I will never know. But this gentle perception remains with me. In his publication *Wonder and Knowledge*, Dr. Robert Pollack stated that a sense of wonder is essential for both scientific discovery and for appreciating the deeper, often unanswerable questions about existence. He emphasized that wonder bridges the gap between the known and the unknown, inspiring both scientific and philosophical exploration. The perception of a ghost can take the form of "presence," an elusive sense that some inexplicable force, benign or otherwise, is nearby. This presence can be perceived as a phantom sighting, sound, smell, touch or an uneasy sense that emerges from deep within us. Ghosts can also take the form of an apparition or of a solid person we can speak with. Only later do we realize that this person was a ghost. The chapters that follow explore the famous and infamous hauntings and ghosts sighting in Iowa, starting with one of the most famous murders and hauntings, the Villisca axe murders.

The Villisca Axe Murders

Iowa is dotted with picturesque small towns nestled among its gently rolling farm fields in southwestern Iowa. One of these towns, Villisca, may have seen better days a century ago, when the railroad was its lifeblood. Still, the city of some two thousand residents is postcard beautiful. It is even more shocking that a mass murder that captured the nation's attention in 1912 is still unsolved and continues to draw visitors not only to the perplexing crime but also, increasingly, to the eerie aspects of the tragedy.

The Villisca axe murder house is probably one of the most famous homes in Iowa because it was featured on such TV shows as *Ghost Adventures*, *Dead Files* and *Kindred Spirits*. Of course, all this television exposure has made it a hot spot for dark tourism, and hundreds of people go there every year. It's $100 plus for an overnight stay in a room, and hundreds more to rent the whole house for the night, although it's a little cheaper during off season.

Josiah B. Moore (Joe), forty-three, and his wife, Sara, thirty-nine, and their four children—Herman, eleven; Katherine, ten; Boyd, seven; and Paul, five—plus two of the children's friends, twelve-year-old Lena Stillinger and eight-year-old Ina Stillinger, were all bludgeoned to death in their sleep by an axe, except for Sara, on whom the killer used a blade.

The Villisca axe murder house with the Grim Reaper. *Photo and drawing by Bruce Walters.*

Bruce Walters and Michael McCarty interviewed documentary filmmaker Kelly Rundle of Fourth Wall Films. The Rundles are award-winning filmmakers, having won five Emmys. He and his wife, Tammy, spent three months at Villisca in 1993 filming the documentary *Villisca: Living with a Mystery*. Kelly was working for Columbia Pictures in the 1990s and took a leave of absence to gather initial film footage for the documentary. This is how Kelly described the night of the murder:

> *It was Children's Day, a Sunday, and at the Presbyterian Church that evening they hosted a special program for children. The service ended a little bit late* [after 9:30 p.m.] *and everybody walked home. The Moore children brought two friends, Lena and Ina Stillinger, home to spend the night. There was absolutely nothing unusual about the night, except that the streetlights failed to come on, and that was the result of an unrelated dispute between the city and the local power company. We described in our film, and it may be true with several other crimes that may be connected, that there were circumstances that made it attractive to the type of person who may have committed the crime: the streetlights were out, and there was a weapon of opportunity—an axe.*
>
> *The axe that had been purchased by someone at the store* [Moore Implement Store, a John Deere franchise] *but was returned for some reason. So, rather than putting it back in stock or trying to sell it, Joe Moore took it home and used it in the coal shed behind the house. It was used to break up coal or chop wood.*

Other eerie elements to the murder include the fact that one mirror downstairs was covered and the parlor door was closed. Most of the windows had shades drawn to the sill. The faces of the victims were also covered.

Despite two grand jury hearings, a slander lawsuit and two murder trials involving a traveling preacher named Reverend George Kelley, who later recanted his confession, the case remains unsolved. (His admission of guilt was creepy as well, but it may have been beaten out of him by the police. The first trial ended in a hung jury, while the second ended in an acquittal.) There were several books written on the subject, but the best is *Fiend Incarnate: Villisca Axe Murders of 1912* by Edgar V. Epperly. The book is rich in information and has more than 190 photographs and diagrams.

Opposite, top: The Villisca axe murder house, where a family of six and two guests were killed in their sleep in 1912. *Courtesy Bruce Walters.*

Opposite, bottom: Second floor at the Villisca House. *Courtesy Bruce Walters.*

Above: The Villisca night visitor of June 10, 1912. *Courtesy Bruce Walters.*

Hoax or Haunted?

Mr. Rundle feels it is a hoax:

> *That's my opinion. There are 4,000 to 5,000 pages of grand jury testimony that just documents the crime scene. And the biggest problem that paranormal people have had with making statements is that they almost always make statements that are contrary to the known historical record.*
>
> *I am not sure hoax is an accurate term. Some may really believe their claims that the house is haunted, in which case it's not an intentional hoax. Darwin Linn* [the man who turned the historic house into a tourist attraction] *told us that he never had any unusual experiences that would lead him to believe it was haunted. But he said his wife Martha believed the house was haunted.*
>
> *While producing our documentary, my wife Tammy and I spent many hours in the house, day and night, and we brought the murder weapon back into the house for the first time since June 10, 1912. We were never haunted by anything other than our own awareness of the tragic events that transpired there.*

Six months after the murder, the house was rented. Many families owned the home until Darwin and Martha Linn bought it in 1994; it was initially just opened for tours. The overnight stays didn't come along until the house was declared "haunted."

Ghost Adventures, *Dead Files* and *Kindred Spirits* all did episodes documenting the different paranormal activities. Books like *A Nightmare in Villisca: Investigating the Haunted Axe Murder House* by Richard Estep and *The Villisca Axe Murders: A House of Horror* by Dominique Bridges, as well as countless magazines and blogs and podcasts, dedicated time and pages to the story.

There have been reports of a shadow figure moving through the house, people have been pushed by an unknown force or watched by unseen eyes, mysterious writings have been seen on bedroom mirrors, there have been disembodied giggles and screams in the night and an unexplained fog has been seen moving from room to room.

Michael McCarty noted, "I really don't want to take sides on if it is hoax or haunted. But I'd like my two cents. Mr. Rundle does make an interesting argument, especially that there were no ghostly encounters for over eight decades from 1912 to 1994."

In the book *Spine-Chilling Murders in Iowa*, author Nick Vulich echoed the same sentiment: "The home changed hands several times over the years. Rick Sprague bought it in the late 1970s and raised his family there. When Mr. Sprague sold the house to Darwin and Martha Linn in 1994, he told the *Des Moines Register* that he'd never seen any ghosts or spirits there."

You see certain patterns with haunted places. There's a tendency toward paranormal activity if it has been renovated. This possibly could have stirred up some activity. Then there's a lot of energy is brought in by giving tours and having people stay overnight; all this talk about the murder over a century ago, night after night, could possibly attract spirits, too.

Vulich continued, "Perhaps the house feels eerie simply because we know what transpired there. Which presents a third option. Regardless, the house is a genuine source of fascination that shows no signs of diminishing. Hoax or haunted, that is only for the reader to decide."

WHERE: 508 EAST 2ND STREET, VILLISCA.

WAPSI WILLY

The Wapsipinicon River is a tributary of the Mississippi River that runs about three hundred miles through the state of Iowa, starting at the southeastern border of Minnesota into the Mississippi. It is commonly called Wapsi River, and there is an Indian folktale behind the name. According to Independence Iowa's website about the river:

> *Wapsi was a young Indian brave and Pinicon was a beautiful Indian maiden. Wapsi was one of the warlike Sioux and Pinicon belonged to the equally hostile tribe of Sac. As fate willed it, they met and fell in love, but strong objections (from both tribes) deterred them from expressing their love to each other. Their love remained strong, and the lovers found a means of communicating their passion and they decided one evening to elope. On the very evening they were preparing to leave, Pinicon's father returned from a hunt and found the two*

Wapsi Willy tombstone at the Skellington Manor. *Courtesy Michael McCarty.*

together. Wapsi fled and Pinicon waited until her father fell fast asleep and she slipped away into the night to find her lover.

Guided by the October moon, the two reunited and Wapsi exclaimed, "Not even death shall ever part us more. Let us fly to my northern home, where parental tyranny can never separate us and we can dwell in peace and harmony until the Great Spirit, 'Gitchie Manitou,' calls us." Just then, they heard footsteps in the distance and realized that Pinicon's father and 3 braves were approaching. They ran in desperate flight away from their chasers. Once they reached the riverbank, there was no time for reconsideration as the murmuring river was singing their funeral chant. Without a word, the devoted lovers clasped in each other's arms and plunged into the river. The enraged father reached the bank only to behold them struggling in the water, sinking and rising and with one last gasp sinking.

The Wapsi Willy legend holds that he and his wife built a cabin in the woods of Clinton County near the Wapsipinicon River. One night, after returning from deer hunting, he was caught up in a terrible storm. It took him several hours to get back home, but when he returned, nothing was there, as his family and the cabin got washed down in a flood. He took a lantern and went up and down the riverbanks looking for them until the day he died. Then his ghost continued the search.

Wapsi Willy animatronic created by and for Skellington Manor, Rock Island. *Photo by Michael McCarty.*

Wapsi Willy is a popular legend, and there was even a restaurant named after the legend in Long Grove that ran from 2016 to 2020. It even had lanterns as part of its décor. David Allan Coe and the southern rock band Molly Hatchet both played there.

When Michael and Penni Steen ran Terror in the Woods, a popular attraction in Donahue, Iowa, they had a tombstone and animatronic ghoul of Wapsi Willy. When their attraction closed, they brought Wapsi Willy with them to their new place in Rock Island, Illinois, that they named Terror in Skellington Manor. Skellington Manor is also haunted—there is a chapter about it in *Eerie Quad Cities*.

Penni explained the legend. "Has to do with the banks of the Wapsipinicon River," she said. "There were these undercurrents that ate away at the ground along the river. Kids would get to close the edge and fall into the river and drown. Parents would tell their kids that Wapsi Willy, this menacing character, would be hiding along the banks and grab them and pull them into the river. It was to scare them from going along the edge of the banks. That's where the original story came from."

WHERE: WAPSIPINICON RIVER.

THE GHOST OF HAZEL

On October 10, 1962, at the old Cedar Rapids Public Library, on the corner of 3rd Avenue and 5th Street Southeast, Hazel McGrew, a frequent patron of the Cedar Rapids Library, was spotted by three library employees when they came down from the balcony level, where newspapers were stored. It wasn't until the afternoon, when the newspaper arrived, that the library staff learned that Hazel had died in a fire the night before.

Hazel had died of smoke inhalation on the evening of October 9 at the three-story, fourteen-unit Mitchell apartment house at 511 A Avenue Northeast. The fire started when someone tossed a cigarette into a trash can by the back door of the building. The blaze was so hot that it prevented the firefighters from entering the building. People had to be rescued via exterior windows. The flames never reached her bedroom, but the smoke did. When one apparition appears after a tragedy, it's called a "crisis apparition" according to local paranormal groups.

Libraries are no strangers to ghosts either. Read about the East Moline Library in *Eerie Quad Cities*.

Where: Was on the corner of 3rd Avenue and 5th Street Southeast. The library is no longer there, but is now the Cedar Rapids Museum of Art, 410 3rd Avenue Southeast.

Farrar Elementary School

In 1919, C.G. Geddes donated six acres of his farm to merge the area's one-room county schoolhouses. In 1922, Farrar Elementary School opened its doors. This seventeen-thousand-square-foot schoolhouse with a $100,000 price tag was built for the students of four counties. In 2002, the school closed its doors. In 2006, it was purchased for use as a banquet room and then resold in 2024.

This building, located across from a graveyard, has seen plenty of spirits over the decades—employees and students hear voices when no one is around, doors slam shut by themselves, unnatural figures walk down the hallways and phantom footsteps are heard.

Several paranormal groups have investigated the building. It was featured on such TV shows as *Kindred Spirits*, *Ghost Hunters*, *My Ghost Story* and *Ghost Stalkers*. It was the subject of the book *A Haunting at Farrar* by Richard Estep and E.E. Benson.

Where: 11125 Northeast 134th Avenue, Maxwell.

Haunted Hospitals

Edinburgh Manor

Mental hospitals are places of fear, pain, abandonment and anger. Some of the patients who enter never see their families or friends again. It is not unusual for such places to become haunted, and Edinburgh is no exception.

In October 2013 and April 2014, paranormal investigator, filmmaker and author Chris Nielson spent five days and nights in an abandoned psychiatric

The Edinburgh Manor in Scotch Grove, a former mental hospital. *Courtesy Bruce Walters.*

home in Scotch Grove called Edinburgh Manor. He wrote about it in a riveting book called *Fear and Fascination in Edinburgh Manor*, containing everything he saw, heard and felt when he was at the isolated mental institution.

Originally, the property was used as the county poor farm. In an interview for the book, Chris Nielson said, "It was established in 1856 and was part of a program that had been, for some time, sweeping the country: the poor farm. A program where countless counties across a still rather young nation would provide a place of residence for their local impoverished. A program that started with the best of intentions…but you know what they say the path to hell is paved with."

There were 230 documented deaths on property. Nielson continued:

> *The building that stands today was constructed in 1911 as The Jones County Home for the Incurably Insane. It closed in 2010 after it lost funding from the state. It was a place I grew fascinated with, then fearful of, then purely loathed. In 2013 I spent the nights and days of October the thirteenth through the eighteenth alone in the building that would one day become Edinburgh Manor.*

Shot from an outside window. The ball was most likely left by a paranormal group for the ghost children to play with. *Courtesy Bruce Walters.*

> *The property saw its share of hardships over the years. When you take into consideration what type of building this was, that can barely surprise you. Over the manor's time of operation, over one hundred and fifty people died on the property and within its walls, at least that's the most recent number I've heard as research continues to be on the building and its history and the history of its inhabitants that were referred to as "inmates" during the poor farm years. Some are still said to be buried on the grounds.*

The haunted institution in eastern Iowa has been featured on TV shows such as *Ghost Adventures*, *Destination Fear* and *Mysterious of the Abandoned*.

Following is Chris Nielson's account of his stay at the Edinburgh Manor:

> *I feel like I need to preface with the fact that, in the end, I grew to love the place. Its decaying walls now feel something like a home to me. I think of the spirits there as an odd extension of my own family. In the end, I feel the paranormal investigator builds relationships with the places and spirits they visit, and although my relationship with Edinburgh Manor had a rocky start to say the least, like any relationship, I had to meet her*

halfway. Let my own ego get sorted out and see her for what she was. A tired old building that needed someone to care about her more than judge her for her turbulent past.

My first introduction to Edinburgh Manor was like how I'm sure most people experience it. You take County Road E-23 through the middle of nowhere, Iowa, and somehow, out of nowhere, this large, serious structure seems to almost manifest between the hills. There's a sense of anxious curiosity as you pull into the long gravel drive, and you step out of your vehicle. That's when you know you're in the presence of something that exists between the worlds of the seen and unseen.

For me, it was a cool October day when I had this realization. I climbed out of my car, looked up at the broad brick façade, and started doing something I still enjoy doing to this day: I walked around the building. I looked up into the long slender windows imagining and half expecting to see some incorporeal form looking back down at me. This is not, in fact, an uncommon occurrence. Many investigators line up for their obligatory group photo on the front steps to find a mysterious extra figure in one of the windows behind them.

After a few laps, we were let inside. I would love to, I will, relive it in my mind, but for a description, I will defer to my book, Fear and Fascination, *for my first impressions going inside:*

> We were first greeted with a large room in front of us, and as we approached, I noticed that the building split in two. To the left, a long, dimly lit hall dyed a soft pink, I assumed from the sunlight coming in through the curtains in the room at the end of the hall. It was the same to the right, but the walls were baby blue. The large amount of peeling paint caught the sunlight coming in from the far window and caused an arrangement of shadows that decorated the walls with a theme of age and decay. I had found my place. Though not intentionally, the inside of the manor seemed to be the set of some horror movies. From a filmmaker's perspective I could appreciate this aesthetic; as the person who would be calling these dilapidated walls home for the next week, I was a little nervous.
>
> Then a new sensation: the eyes. The eyes of countless not just seeing you but taking notice.

Heads poking out of every door, some were simply inquisitive, others seemed to make me feel aware of just how much I was intruding. I was, after all, an unannounced guest in their home.

The place had certainly felt intense, but I was much more curious than I was afraid of it. There was a tour, I remember. A tour that was somewhat abruptly ended when the manor's owner, my cameraman, and I all heard an indisputable and thoroughly blood-chilling scream in the basement. This was my introduction to Edinburgh Manor; if we were continuing on that relationship building metaphor I touched on earlier, this was my first date with Edinburgh, and there were several red flags that I was choosing to ignore considering I was about to call these walls home for the next week.

This disembodied screaming is not at all an uncommon phenomenon. Many investigators have reported the same wailing from an unseen source. An almost cliché horror movie style scream. One that comes from no particular direction, but everywhere at once.

As someone who regularly presents on my book Fear and Fascination, *I have had the, to me, very cool pleasure of hearing other people's stories of the place. Some things I'm told are new stories to me, but what will never cease to amaze me are how many times these things line up. People who should have no business having the same story somehow do.*

For me, Edinburgh Manor is a place that has produced some of my most profound findings as well as personal experiences as a paranormal investigator. Lengthy *bouts of audible voices as well as electronic voice phenomena including the inexplicable sound of a baby crying. Loud bangs from doors slamming shut or some other unseen source; what some may refer to as poltergeist phenomenon. Undiagnosable spikes in electromagnetic fields. Cold spots. The ever-mysterious shadow people peering out of doorways down the long halls. What sets this old, weathered brick structure apart for me though is that this is the place I saw with my own eyes the "holy grail" for paranormal investigators: the full-bodied apparition.*

From the pages of *Fear and Fascination*:

I had turned to the chair that I had just been sitting in. After that, as I turned, my eyes went into the large common room next door over. Standing in the middle of the room was a little girl. She was about 8 or 9.

I couldn't explain why, but I knew she was the little girl I had seen on my first day and had played peek-a-boo with me just last night. She wasn't looking at me though. It was as though I didn't exist at all. She was looking straight through me.

She wore an older style of nightgown. Her dark blonde hair came down to her shoulders and her bangs were cut to frame her face. It was undoubtedly the face of a child, but there was a strange maturity to her eyes as she stared.

This was of course all processed very quickly because as soon as I saw the child my instincts told me to jump. Once my eyes were able to refocus on the spot where she stood, she was gone.

Again, I was frustrated by my startled response. The brain stem reacts how it does, how it has since before we climbed out of the trees as apes, in a way that it believes to be in its own self-interest. This is good for survival. A difficult hurdle when trying to cope with a dead girl appearing before you.

She was, is, a little girl that I and many others would come to know as Susie. Little of her personal history is known. All we can know

Another photo taken from an outside window at Edinburgh Manor. *Courtesy Bruce Walters.*

for sure is that her interactions are innocent and damn near cute in an environment that almost seems to contradict such behavior. A small, shimmering light in a place that otherwise might be menacing. During my week-long stay, I give her credit personally for pulling me back from what could have been a very dark place.

And where there is light, there must also be that darkness, for without it, there is no balance. Where there is a Susie, there must be "The Joker." "The Joker" likes to mess with people—moving objects, making eerie noises, even scratching visitors. It lurks in the basement, feeding off fear. Some say it's more than just a lost soul, something darker.

For me, I can only speculate based on my hundreds of hours of experience in Edinburgh Manor, but I think I have this guy nailed down. There is a room past the notorious padded cell. An old maintenance room that, to some, may be easily overlooked. In this room I have encountered what I can only describe as: a cantankerous old bastard with a bad attitude. A maintenance man who has lingered around "his space" for much too long. Many may take his uncomfortable presence for something "demonic" or otherwise in nature, but in one guy's experience, to quote a great teacher of mine, "a-hole in life, a-hole in death."

These are just two examples of the many personalities that call the manor home. It was a home to the old, the confused, the schizophrenic, and the depressed. It was a sanctuary to some, a prison to others. It was a place where good people went to do god's work and did their best to care for the people that couldn't take care of themselves.

In the end, Edinburgh Manor, no matter its sentimental value to me, may just be a building—brick and mortar, slowly losing the fight against time and the elements. But it's what lingers inside that stays with you. The dark corners, the peeling walls, the distant echoes of lives lived and lost. It's not just the spirits. It's a reminder of what happens when we turn our backs on people. It's the hope of knowing there are good souls out there that find life's purpose in caring for these people.

For some, it was refuge. For others, a place to simply be disregarded and hidden away with the other "undesirables" of society: the orphans, the elderly, the mentally ill. A sanctuary. A hunting ground. A place with a history as deep and complex as the people that called Edinburgh Manor home.

WHERE: 13241 E23 COUNTY HOME ROAD, MONTICELLO.

Independence State Mental Hospital

The Independence State Mental Hospital (ISMH) is an ominous-looking facility—a gargantuan structure with tan bricks and mortar and pillar columns, along with a labyrinth of tunnels that connect the buildings together underground and a graveyard too. The institution has a gruesome and dark history, including lobotomies, electric shock therapy and hydrotherapy tubs.

This second state asylum was built in 1873 to relieve the overcrowding of the Mount Pleasant State Hospital. It was to be used for the mental ill, the criminally insane, the elderly, alcoholics and drug addicts. It cost $800,000 and took ten years to construct. It was designed by Stephen Vaugh Shipman, who was also the architect for other mental institutions in Illinois and Wisconsin.

Most of this psychiatric hospital in Buchanan County is currently in use, and there is also a museum on the grounds. The older parts of the hospital are closed off but are occasionally opened for school tours. People have reported hearing faint whispers when no one is around or feeling cold drafts; they have the unshakable feeling that someone is watching them from the dark, empty spaces. Disembodied voices and even screams have frightened visitors.

The website Mysterious Heartland said of the Independence, "Apparitions of former staff and patients are seen in the buildings and on the grounds around the hospital." The site ranked the Independence State Mental Hospital as the "sixth most haunted hospital in the Midwest."

The ISMH was also the inspiration for the Silver Springs Psychiatric Facility in the science fiction/dark adventure novel *Out of Time* by Michael McCarty and Connie Corcoran Wilson.

WHERE: 2277 IOWA AVENUE, INDEPENDENCE.

Mercy Hospital

Bret Grimes, author of *The St. Elizabeth's Hospital Fire in Iowa*, said:

> *Somebody that I know that used to work in the basement of Mercy Hospital* [now Genesis West, the site of the St. Elizabeth's fire] *in the 1990s told me a story about how in their department, they*

Top: The grave site at the former St. Elizabeth Hospital, now the MercyOne Genesis Medical Center West Central Park. *Courtesy Bruce Walters.*

Bottom: Rose Wichman was supposedly haunting the basement of the hospital. *Courtesy Bruce Walters.*

would oftentimes have papers getting shuffled and doors that would get slammed (when nobody else was around) that they had no reasonable explanation to as to why that was happening.

They had believed that there was a ghost that had something to do with the St. Elizabeth fire. They named the ghost Rosie. And then one of the workers contacted a priest out of the Chicagoland area. Chicago is where the Sisters of Mercy came from. The priest...came out to perform an exorcism. The priest came out, everything stopped, and they didn't have any issues.

I later told that person that Rose Wichman was one of the 16 that was buried at the gravesite at Mercy Hospital. I have no reason to believe that she was lying to me, but it was kind of eerie.

WHERE: MERCY HOSPITAL IS NOW MERCYONE GENESIS MEDICAL CENTER, CENTRAL PARK, 1351 WEST CENTRAL PARK, DAVENPORT.

HAUNTED HOTELS AND INNS

Hotel Julien

Iowa's oldest hotel is also one of the most haunted. It was built in 1839 with four stories by wealthy merchant Peter Waple and named the Waple House. It was sold in 1854 and renovated to have eighty rooms, with the name changed to the Hotel Julien after the founder of the city, Julien Dubuque. In 1866, it was bought by W.W. Woodworth for $30,000; more stories were added.

The giant mirror in the lobby was salvaged from the Ziegfeld Theatre in New York City. Legendary performers such as W.C. Fields, Will Rogers, Louise Brooks, Fanny Brice, Bob Hope and more caught their last glance in this mirror before heading to the Ziegfeld stage.

More than $30 million was spent on the interior and exterior renovations in the hotel over the years; it now has 133 rooms. President Abraham Lincoln, Buffalo Bill Cody, Mark Twain and gangster Al Capone have all stayed here. Capone, in fact, was a frequent guest at the hotel, and he occupied the eighth floor and had guards posted there. If he ordered room service, the food would have to be given to his guards, as the servers weren't allowed on the floor. He liked the fact that he could see people

The staircase at the Hotel Julien. *Courtesy Bruce Walters.*

The eighth floor at the Hotel Julien in Dubuque. Al Capone would rent out the whole floor when he stayed there. *Courtesy Bruce Walters.*

traveling over the Wagon Bridge from Illinois from that floor. The gangster also made use of the underground garage, which concealed his arrival and departures.

Staff and guests have reported seeing the gangster's spirit, usually walking on the upper floors. He's said to be dressed in 1920s and 1930s clothing, including a nice suit and a fedora, with a scar on the side of his face. One man commented to his wife, "Hey, that man looks like Al Capone." When she turned to look, there was no one there.

Other entities include a female apparition floating five feet off the floor near the staircases and other areas of the hotel. The freight elevator also seems to have a mind of its own.

One lady stepped out of the shower and found the bathroom filled with steam. She opened the door to let the steam dissipate and was frightened by the sight of a man in her room. She screamed, and the stranger disappeared in front of her.

A couple was making love in the dark when the lamp on the bed stand suddenly turned on by itself.

WHERE: 200 MAIN STREET, DUBUQUE.

Hotel Ottumwa

Built in 1917 and then closed in 1973, this building sat vacant for almost a decade until the Schwartz family acquired and renovated the historic hotel. Bruce Walters said that the lobby looked like something out of *The Shining*. The Hotel Ottumwa still has a retro sophistication, historical charm and ghosts too.

The basement (formerly a ballroom) sees the most paranormal activity. Apparitions include a woman in white, frequently seen in the lower levels of the hotel. A strange man's face is seen peering in the darkness, and another man follows people down the hallways. Shadow figures are seen in various areas. Spooky sounds and heavy breathing are heard when no one is around, and talking is heard in unoccupied rooms.

WHERE: 107 2ND STREET EAST, OTTUMWA.

Top: The Hotel Ottumwa lobby. *Courtesy Bruce Walters.*

Bottom: The landing that goes to the basement at the Hotel Ottumwa. Ghosts have been seen in this area. *Courtesy Bruce Walters.*

Mason House Inn Bed-and-Breakfast

This structure was built by Mormon craftsmen from Nauvoo, Illinois, in 1846 as a place to rest for steamboat travelers. In 1857, Lewis Mason and his wife bought the place and changed the name to the Phoenix Hotel, but everyone called it the Mason House.

This three-story brick structure has a long and twisted history. Lewis Mason died of diphtheria in 1862 in the house. His daughter Mary Mason Clark died of a heart attack on the third floor in 1911. It was a makeshift hospital during the Civil War, and one doctor died in his own office. In 1913, it was turned into a tuberculosis sanitarium.

Room 7 is a careful replica of the 1870 President Abraham Lincoln room at the White House, including a guest bed reproduction. It is decorated with Lincoln's books and memorabilia as a tribute to the sixteenth president.

It might not be too surprising that Lincoln's spirit has been seen there. So have about three hundred other ghosts. *The Today Show* called the Mason House Inn "one of the most haunted bed and breakfasts in America."

Room 5 holds an apparition of a young boy named George who knocks on doors and moves things around. Room 7 is the home of a spirit named Mr. Knapp, who was stabbed to death after accidentally crawling into the

The Mason Inn was called "one of the most haunted bed and breakfasts in America" on *The Today Show*. *Courtesy Bruce Walters.*

wrong bed. Room 8 sees a manifestation of a floating head. The specter of an elderly woman is known to walk the empty rooms on the third floor.

The Mason House has been the site of several paranormal investigations but won't permit Ouija boards on the premises.

Where: 21982 Hawk Drive, Keosauqua.

Hotel Blackhawk

The ghosts of Cary Grant and others have been reported to haunt this hotel. To find out more, read *Ghosts of Quad Cities*.

Haunted Cemeteries

Hickory Hill Cemetery

The Little Girl Apparition

In the spring of 2024, Cindy and Michael McCarty and comedian Shannon Trimble and his wife, Veronique Fernandez, went to the Hickory Hill Cemetery. This is Michael's recollection of the graveyard and the haunted legend there:

> *I heard about Hickory Hill Cemetery in Charlotte for years. I became extremely interested in the place around the release of* Ghosts of the Quad Cities *in the fall of 2019. I saw a video on YouTube on supernatural dares called "Do Not Touch the Gate at the Haunted Hickory Hill Cemetery." Chad Lewis and Kevin Nelson went to the cemetery, talked about the legend of a ghostly little girl who will point and say "get off" if you touch the gate entrance. There are also reports of ghost babies crying during both the day and night.*
>
> *I put it on my to-do list and thought of possibly including it for* Eerie Quad Cities *but ended scratching it off the list in the end. Although in Clinton County, I thought the graveyard was too far from the areas in the book.*
>
> *Years later, my friends Shannon and Veronique and I were talking about Hickory Hill and thought we could visit it after going to Tycoga*

The entrance to Hickory Hill Cemetery in Charlotte. *Courtesy Michael McCarty.*

Winery & Distillery in DeWitt. Everyone sampled a glass of wine; I had a wine slushie.

We came from DeWitt, Iowa, into Charlotte. The cemetery is really off the beaten path, between farmland and located in a wooded area up a gravel trail about a quarter of a mile from the main road. It is easy to drive by. Lucky for us, Veronique had been there before.

The cemetery is on the top of the hill, on the left side. It is well maintained but also very secluded among the trees.

There are around 50 memorials, and it is said to be around 100 people buried there, many unmarked.

We all walked to the gate. I took photos of the creepy sign. Veronique announced that "we come to pay respect and will do no harm, and can we have permission to enter?" We waited for a few moments and opened the gate and entered.

Veronique had brought a gift, a plastic ball, and threw it on the ground for the ghost girl to play with. There was no activity, but the place did seem a lot friendlier after that.

Hickory Hill is called a "Pioneer Cemetery," and it is very old. There are tombstones and grave markers from as early as 1876 and

> *1877, 1895 and 1899 up until the 1920s. There are several children and infant graves as well.*
>
> *We stayed at the old rural cemetery for about a half hour, looking at the different tombstones before leaving.*

GRAVE ROBBERY

Local historian and author John Brassard Jr. noted this about what happened to one of the grave sites at Hickory Hill:

> *The ATV riders that cool spring morning were confronted with a surprising reality.*
>
> *As they rode past Hickory Hill, they noticed that one of the graves had been dug up. The Clinton County Sheriff's Department was notified and began a prompt investigation.*
>
> *A twin grave, belonging to a husband and wife within the Illeman family plot, had been completely opened. Although the vaults were clearly visible and the handles to them had been uncovered, neither had been opened.*
>
> *Investigators discovered that twine had been run between the gravestone and some nearby trees. Not wanting to attract unwanted attention, the perpetrators could hang blankets or some other covering around the site to help keep their work light hidden. The perpetrators had left muddy footprints on the vaults themselves, and a broken shovel that was assumed to have been used in the excavation was found in the area. And why did someone do all of this? The Sheriff's Department had theories, but no strong leads.*
>
> *It might be a case of grave robbing. Perhaps the grave had been excavated because the plot looked like the biggest and most important one there, making it the most likely to have money and jewelry. Surviving relatives of the Illemans however, informed investigators that the deceased couple hadn't had much money and there probably wouldn't be anything of significant value buried with them.*
>
> *Simple vandalism was another possibility. Although there weren't any gravestones broken or knocked over, smaller objects from the monuments, such as crosses, had been seemingly removed. However, the grave was about six feet deep and ten feet wide. The conditions were muddy, and care was taken to hide their activities from the road. Wouldn't it have just been easier to break a few stones and walk away?*
>
> *In the end, it was all speculation with no clear reason. No one was ever caught for the crime. The graves were refilled, and things returned to normal. After a while, the whole incident was forgotten by many.*

Family plot that was vandalized; a relative had a concrete pad poured over the vault to prevent any future disturbances. *Courtesy Veronique Fernandez.*

There is, however, an interesting side note to this story:

After the issue had settled down, a relative of one of the other families buried at Hickory Hill decided that his ancestor would never be disturbed like the Illemans had been.

One day, he began to pour a concrete pad over the graves of his relatives. The pad grew in size until it became big enough to park a car on. It may not have been a foolproof method of deterring someone from digging up those remains, but they were going to have to try a whole lot harder now.

The Illemans—Maria Gohlmann, "Meda" (1864–1921), and Mathias H., "Father" (1855–1927)—may finally rest in peace again.

WHERE: NORTH OF 340TH AND HIGHWAY 136, CHARLOTTE, IOWA.

Greenwood Cemetery

Mark Manuel, program director and radio host of BIG 106 FM in the Quad Cities, has heard more than a few ghost stories in his time. A listener told Mr. Manuel one involving Greenwood Cemetery: "If you walk down the center of the cemetery you will hear the sound of footsteps running at you, but when you turn to look at the direction the noise is coming from you will see nothing. A strong feeling of being watched and followed is felt. Even reports of a strange scream that seems to come from the other side of the cemetery but can hurt your ears at the same time."

WHERE: 1814 LUCAS STREET, MUSCATINE.

Oak Hill Cemetery

The legend goes that a young Czech girl named Tillie passed away while her parents were passing through Cedar Rapids. It is said that she wanders the cemetery at night holding a flickering candle and that she has been known to pull people inside mausoleums.

The story can be traced back to one of the groundskeepers at the cemetery, who made it up to scare his coworker. However, there really was a Tillie at the graveyard. Tillie Krcmar, a ten-year-old Czech girl, was buried in the potter's field section of Oak Hill Cemetery. The Krcmars lost two of their children to diphtheria in 1893.

Oak Hill Cemetery was established in 1854.

WHERE: 1705 MOUNT VERNON ROAD SOUTHEAST, CEDAR RAPIDS.

Pleasant Ridge Cemetery

Pleasant Ridge Cemetery is commonly known as "13 Steps" because that is the number of steps leading up the hill into the graveyard. Ghostly voices have been recorded as electronic voice phenomena. A phantom dog has been seen. There is a story of a witch being buried at the cemetery. Human-like shapes have appeared and disappeared at random.

WHERE: LOCATED ON LEWIS BOTTOMS ROAD, PALOS.

Hazel Green Cemetery

Five miles south of Ackley, out in the county, is the Hazel Green Cemetery, which was established in 1863. The residents have reported strange and unexplained phenomena at the graveyard, including an elderly woman rocking a baby at the gazebo, orbs, loud banging noises and eerie howling. It is a well-kept and well-maintained cemetery. People have been known to leave flowers for the old lady and infant at the white gazebo.

WHERE: GRAVEL ROAD 155, ONE-FOURTH MILE EAST OF U AVENUE IN ACKLEY.

Stone Chair Angels: Union Cemetery and Riverside Cemetery

Two stone chair statues in two different cemeteries are said to be cursed.

Chad Lewis, coauthor of *The Iowa Road Guide to Haunted Locations*, said in an interview with the *Times Republican* newspaper about the cursed chair at the Riverside Cemetery in Marshalltown, "People say that when you sit in the Cursed Chair or the Devil's Chair in the Riverside Cemetery, you'll be cursed or die, have misfortune, mishap or bad luck."

The same legend is true with the cursed chair at Union Cemetery in Guthrie Center, although this one is the more famous chair. One of the reasons for its notoriety is that the chair is situated between two rows but is unmarked and doesn't belong to any of the plots.

Iowa PBS offered an explanation: "In the nineteenth century, graveyards included a chair for comfort for the mourners. The purpose of these chairs fell out of fashion over the time and the urban legends about them began to spread over time."

WHERE: RIVERSIDE CEMETERY, 611 NORTH CENTER STREET, MARSHALLTOWN, AND UNION CEMETERY, 1366 NORTH STREET, GUTHRIE CENTER.

EERIE ANGEL STATUES

Black Angel: Ruth Anne Dodge Memorial

A winding road that leads upward to the bluffs that overlook the Missouri River Valley ends at a rising grassy crest adjacent to Fairview Cemetery in Council Bluffs. Here stands a cast bronze figure of a winged angel. Its haunting, austere figure is larger than life (eight and a half inches tall). The angel represents a recurring, eerie dream that possessed the wife of railroad magnate Major General Grenville Dodge. After his death in 1916, her own health rapidly declined.

According to the article "The Black Angel of Council Bluffs" from the Spiritual Travels website, "One night, she had a dream, so vivid it was more in the nature of a vision. She was standing on a rocky shore when a boat approached her out of the mist. It was carrying an angel, tall and beautiful, who held a basin of water."

The sculpture was created by artist Daniel Chester French; the base and pool were designed by architect Henry Bacon. They were also working on the Lincoln Memorial in Washington, D.C., at the same time. *Courtesy Bruce Walters.*

The wings of the Black Angel, Ruth Anne Dodge Memorial, Council Bluffs. *Courtesy Bruce Walters.*

"Drink," the angel said. "I bring you both a promise and a blessing."

Ruth Anne declined the offer, later telling her daughter Anne, "I felt unworthy, and it seemed to me it would be presumption on my part to partake of anything so wonderfully pure, so heavenly, so spiritual."

Then the dream came to her again a few days later, the same as before. Once again Ruth Anne told the angel no. But when she had the dream a third time, she accepted the offer of water, and in the process, she felt that she'd been "transformed into a new and glorious spiritual being." A few days later, Ruth Anne Dodge died.

The sculpture was created by artist Daniel Chester French; the base and pool were designed by architect Henry Bacon. While this memorial was being made (1916–20), this same team of creators was working on the Lincoln Memorial in Washington, D.C.

This uncanny story has an unsettling twist. The woman who posed for the angel, Audrey Munson, also served as the model for many of America's great artists and starred on Broadway and in silent films. However, she was committed to a mental asylum by her mother fifteen years after serving as the model of the angel. She would remain at the asylum, the St. Lawrence State Hospital of the Insane in New York, for sixty-five years until her death at the age of 104. For twenty-five years, she had no visitors. A gravestone was placed on Munson's grave twenty years after death, one hundred years after Ruth Anne Dodge was laid to rest in a mausoleum near her memorial in 1916.

Council Bluffs, Iowa, was named after a meeting that took place in the area between the Lewis and Clark Expedition and the Otoe and Missouria Native American tribes in 1804.

Where: North 2nd Street and Lafayette Avenue, Council Bluffs.

The Black Angel

In the heart of Oakland Cemetery in Iowa City, there is an ominous and mysterious sculpture of an angel with her gaze cast downward. How or when it became black only adds to its mystery.

Vernon Trollinger wrote in *Haunted Iowa City* about the statue, "The Black Angel—or the Feldwert Monument, as it formally known has been Iowa City's alter ego for a century. A nine and half a feet tall statue looms atop a granite pedestal a little over three feet high. Mournfully looks down, its wings drooping its arms stretched wide in a gesture suggesting somber surprise and warning."

Such deadly warnings as "Any girl kissed near her in the moonlight will die within six months" or "Touching the Angel at midnight on Halloween means death within seven years" have gathered like the shadow under its drooping wings since it arrived in Iowa City on a flatcar in 1912.

Bruce Walters said, "When I last saw the sculpture in 2024, a few objects had been left on its base, including the tarot card The Moon, which

The Black Angel of Oakland Cemetery in Iowa City. *Courtesy Bruce Walters.*

symbolically represents 'unveiling secrets.'" There was also was a battered penny lying tails up, which has been associated with evil or bad luck.

The monument was commissioned by Teresa Dolezal Feldevert, who was born in 1836 in present-day Czech Republic. She trained as a physician at the University of Vienna, but her medical certification was not accepted in the United States, and she served as a midwife throughout the remainder of her life. When she died in 1924, her ashes were buried along with the ashes of her first husband, who preceded her in death.

The prominent words on the stone base, "RODINA FELDEVERTOVA," simply mean the "Feldevert family." Their son's gravestone is to the side. The Bohemian inscription on a side of the base has been translated as, "The sun and clouds stood above my journey. There were tough and joyful days in my life. You did my work just to make the world better. You fold your hands and your head goes down. Your spirit flies away where everlasting reward is waiting for you after hardship."

The sculptor was Mario Korbel, a Czech artist who lived in Chicago. His figurative work is somber and often titled with a simple description, although some are titled "Night" or "Nocturne." They are consistent in tone with the

The Moon Tarot card on the base of the Black Angel. *Courtesy Bruce Walters.*

Black Angel, which has a melancholy and expressionist quality reminiscent of Edvard Munch's paintings. The angel is genuinely eerie.

To learn more about the Black Angel of Riverside Cemetery in Moline, read *Ghosts of the Quad Cities*.

Where: Oakland Cemetery, 1000 Brown Street, Iowa City.

The Blue Angel

The Blue Angel is a statue with a legend attached to it. Reports say that back in the 1950s, she was thought of as the benevolent spirit of the cemetery, protecting it from vandals. Sometime since then, tales about her have become more sinister. She is said to have once held a rose; if

The Blue Angel of Greenwood Cemetery, Muscatine. *Courtesy Bruce Walters.*

you looked at her and she dropped the rose, you were doomed to die. Reports say that her hand was cut off so she couldn't hurt anyone, but at night, they say her hand is still here, glowing and holding the rose. On her mausoleum, there are two cobalt blue stained-glass windows, one on the east side and one on the west; when the sun shines through the windows, it gives her white gypsum a blue tint.

Mark Manuel, program director and radio host of BIG 106 FM in the Quad Cities, has heard more than a few ghost stories in his time. A listener told Mr. Manuel one involving the Blue Angel: "The Blue Angel is a statue in the Greenwood Cemetery who used to hold a rose. When approaching the angel, you will see the sky turn blood red, and when you look at the trees—because the angel is set back all by itself in a cove—the short side of the trees will be swaying and the tall side will not."

Bruce Walters noted, "If we think of the cemetery's entrance gates as the front, the mausoleum is in the back corner, overlooking the city from a bluff. Unfortunately, photos lose a lot [of impact] when it's black-and-white instead of being in color."

WHERE: 1814 LUCAS STREET, MUSCATINE.

TERROR BRIDGES

The Swinging Bridge

A bridge is a constructed structure spanning an obstacle such a river or lake, valley, road or railroad with a pathway to get a cross. Some people have a fear of bridges because of the heights, the fear that it might collapse, anxiety about drowning or accidentally falling off.

When coauthor Michael McCarty was a kid, his dad would joke when going over the Rock Island Arsenal bridge when the train was above: "The train is going to fall down on your heads." All the McCarty kids would scream. But who hasn't crossed a rusty old bridge or a rickety wooden bridge and wondered, "Is this safe enough to cross?"

The Swinging Bridge in Columbus Junction is one of those bridges, and it has a haunted past. The sign says it all:

The Swinging Bridge
Lovers Leap Bridge

1886—The first bridge of barrel staves and wire was soon replaced by one built on wooden stilts.
1902—The first bridge was condemned for safety reasons.
1904—A swinging bridge was built to the length of 150 feet.
1920—The swinging bridge collapsed with two persons aboard, neither was injured.
1922—The present bridge was erected to span 262 feet.
1954—The flooring and steel cable were refurbished.

Did a Lovesick Maiden Leap to Her Death? The Trees Know, and They Won't Tell.

Here's a little more information about the 1920 story. According to the book *Secret Iowa* by Megan Bannister, "In 1920 teenage brothers Lew and

The sign by the Swinging Bridge of Columbus Junction. *Courtesy Michael McCarty.*

Jesse Tisor were crossing the bridge when the planks below them suddenly gave away. Miraculously, the brothers landed on the ground, still standing upright, and walked away completely unscathed."

There are two ways to get to the bridge. You can park at the foot of the hill, and there is a well-maintained trail named Possum Hollow that goes to the top where the bridge is located. On top of the hill, on 3rd Street, the bridge is next to two signs with a small parking area.

This is not for the faint of heart or weak-kneed people. This bridge is built over a ravine that is eight stories high, and it moves when you walk across it.

According to legend, and reported on Atlas Obscura and in the *Des Moines Register*, a lovesick Native American maiden threw herself to the bottom of the ravine to end her grief. It is said that she was buried at the bottom, and her wails can be heard when crossing the bridge when no one is around.

Where: 303 Oak Street, Columbus Junction.

Bannwell Terror Bridge

Just outside Fort Dodge is one of the oldest haunted bridges in Iowa. It is so old that no one is certain when it was built. Some say 1890s, while others say it was even earlier than that. But residents do agree on one thing: it is haunted.

It is known as Tara Bridge for a nearby town that no longer exists, but it is more commonly called Terror Bridge. It's a one-lane bridge over the Union Pacific Railroad tracks. It was officially named Bannwell Bridge and described as the "220th Street Overpass" and a "pony truss bridge."

There are several ghost stories about the railroad below. The most famous involves a mother who took her three children to watch a train pass. As the locomotive got closer, she pushed each child over the bridge, one after another, and then jumped to her own death as well.

The Haunted Destination website warns drivers going over the bridge to "roll up the windows and lock the doors before crossing. Otherwise, the woman's spirit will try to pull you out of the vehicle and throw you over, just as she did with her children. Those brave enough to get out of their cars have reported hearing voices, seeing orbs, and, at times, hearing a woman moaning from beneath the overpass."

Where: 1981–99 Fairbanks Avenue, Fort Dodge.

Creepy Covered Bridge

The Bridges of Madison County is a novel written by Robert James Waller that was published in 1992; it became a bestseller, putting the area on the map as a national tourist spot. In 1995, Clint Eastwood directed a film adaptation of the novel and also starred as photographer Robert Kincaid, who takes photos of the covered bridges. He meets farm wife Francesca Johnson, played by Meryl Streep. They soon embark on a romantic affair.

There are six of these picturesque bridges in Madison County. They were built with these covers to protect the timber from the elements and reduce maintenance costs.

The Roseman Covered Bridge is in Winterset, the same town where actor John Wayne was born. The bridge was built in 1883 and is 225 feet long and 15.5 feet high. Vehicle traffic is no longer allowed, but foot traffic is permitted. It is also known as the "Haunted Bridge" because of many unexplained occurrences.

There are two local legends surrounding the Roseman. A young couple met at the covered bridge because the girl's father forbade them to see each other. One night, the young man crossed the bridge on his horse to meet his sweetheart, but instead he was chased by her father and his friends. Only the horse made it out alive.

The Roseman Bridge, the haunted bridge of *The Bridges of Madison County*. *Courtesy Bruce Walters.*

Under the Roseman Bridge in Winterset. *Courtesy Bruce Walters.*

The other tale, from 1892, concerns an escaped prisoner from the county jail who was trapped on the bridge by the sheriff's deputies; out of nowhere, the man completely disappeared from sight.

Over the years, unexplained or muffled laughter could be heard coming from the bridge. Others reported hearing wagon wheels going through the tunnel. Cold spots have been noticed in the center of the bridge. And people witness their dog's hackles rise once inside.

Where: 2451 Elderberry Avenue, Winterset.

Haunted Museums and Art Galleries

The Ham House

Dubuque, Iowa, is one of the oldest cities in the state and is among the oldest settlements west of the Mississippi River. French-Canadian fur trader Julien Dubuque was one of the first settlers in the area. When he arrived in 1785, the Mesquakie (Fox) Indians occupied the region, which included a number of lead mines.

Dubuque also has its share of eerie locations and ghost stories. According to the Haunted Dubuque website, "The Ham House has been reported to be haunted for over 150 years."

The *Des Moines Register* wrote this about the Ham House: "This building is said to be one of the most haunted places in Dubuque. It was once a large private residence but is now a museum. People have experienced classic encounters such as cold breezes, strange voices and chills running down people's spines. Several of the caretakers have reported objects mysteriously out of place and lights flickering. There have even been reports of eerie cries coming from the servant's house, the master bedroom, and the nursery." Other eerie events include phantom footsteps, moving furniture and music coming from a broken organ.

Mathias Ham (1805–1888) was born and raised in Tennessee. He made and lost several fortunes over his lifetime. His success from his early mining days in Dubuque helped pay for the mansion. The place is a hodgepodge of styles—mid-Victorian with Tudor wooden arches supported by octagonal columns.

The Ham House in Dubuque has been haunted for more than 150 years. *Courtesy Bruce Walters.*

Front entrance to the Ham House. *Courtesy Bruce Walters.*

Ham, along with his wife, Zerelda, and their six children, lived at the residence. Over the years, several family members died there, including Mathias and Zerelda and daughter May. There was also an intruder. Someone broke inside the home and was shot by daughter Sarah.

Where: 2241 Lincoln Avenue, Dubuque.

Dakota City Historical Museum

The Dakota City Historical Museum was built on December 30, 1976, to expand on its previous space in the overcrowded basement of the city building.

The DCHM comprises a schoolhouse, a log cabin and a Victorian farmhouse and tells the history of Humboldt County and its people. Shadows are seen, and lights turn on and off by themselves. Local legends says that a man drowned in the river next to the museum and that he still haunts the place today.

Where: 905 1st Avenue North, Dakota City.

Mississippi Spoon Gallery

A one-of-a-kind museum in Davenport, opened in August 2023, may have more than just spoons in it. Strange and unexplained things have been happening at the souvenir spoon gallery.

Owner and curator Cammie Pohl's great-grandmother Amelia Watts gave her three boxes before she left for the army in 1987. "She told me not to open them until I got married or bought my first home," Mrs. Pohl said. The boxes sat in storage as she served her country.

After Cammie and her husband, Randy, bought their first home, "I opened the boxes and was taken by the beauty and intricacy of the silver spoons." This started her passion for collecting spoons from antique shops and flea markets from coast to coast and twenty-nine countries too. She has twenty-seven thousand polished spoons—ten thousand are featured in the gallery—with some more than a century old.

Some of her prized possessions include spoons gifted to queens from Victoria to Elizabeth II, given to them by the silversmith who created them. "My great-grandmother had attended the St. Louis World's Fair in 1904 and attended the World's Fair of 1933," Mrs. Pohl said. "And I started collecting Expo spoons. We won a blue ribbon at the Mississippi Valley Fair." She has won multiple blue ribbons over the years.

She also has spoons from all over the globe, including Italy, Egypt and China. About 50 percent of the spoons are made from silver; others are pewter, and a few are even stained-glass. One of her most visually striking items is a "spoondelier," a chandelier made up of gleaming tableware utensils hanging from the ceiling.

She also has a spoon commemorating the Salem witch trial created by Daniel Low in 1891. "That started the whole craze," she stated. She also has several items with Iowa connections, including a spoon from the Independence State Mental Hospital and Black Hawk spoons.

Some of the eerie occurrences that have happened at the spoon gallery include spoons disappearing from their display case and reappearing in completely different areas days later. Strange clinking noises are heard. Spoons fall after being securely fastened, and a visiting medium claimed that there was a ghost in Cammie's office. "I have absolutely have no belief in that stuff," Mrs. Pohl said. "But I can't explain it either. I am a little nervous to think that there is a ghost."

Ghost or not, the Mississippi Spoon Gallery is well worth checking out to see souvenir spoons of gorgeous artistry and history depicting an era gone

An 1820 dragon spoon from China at the Mississippi Spoon Gallery. *Courtesy Michael McCarty.*

by. Cammie gives tours of the museum. Weird things often happen at the beginning of the day, and people have witnessed spoons hanging upside down and in a locked case.

WHERE: 902 EAST RIVER DRIVE, DAVENPORT.

German American Heritage Center and Museum

As written in *Quad Cities Beer*, according to the German American Heritage Center and Museum's website, "In the mid-to-late 1800s, millions of German citizens left their homeland for America. Scott County, Iowa, where the first passenger railroad crossed the Mississippi River, was the 'Ellis Island' of the Midwest for many of these immigrants. Upon arrival, thousands stayed in the Standard Hotel, built in the 1860 and located on West 2nd and Gaines Streets in downtown Davenport."

The building was built by John Brus and opened in 1862 as the Germania House, a gasthaus (guest house) for immigrants. In 1876, it was bought by John Frederick Miller and renamed the Miller Hotel. He was a German immigrant who had been a manufacturer in the city since the 1850s. Miller also operated the restaurant, the billiard room and the saloon in the hotel until 1889. The hotel was used at this time by Scott County farmers when they came to Davenport. The hotel's name was changed several times in the twentieth century. It became the Arcade Hotel around 1906, the Henry Blessing Boarding House around 1917 and the Standard Hotel from 1924 to 1995.

The German American Heritage Center and Museum purchased the building in 1995 and restored it by 1999, reopening it to the public in May 2000.

The GAHC has permitted several paranormal groups to investigate the location over the years. Michael McCarty interviewed Clare Tobin, assistant director and curator, and Jolene Harvey, who had been a volunteer since 2017 after the organization Whispering Souls did its investigation. "There's three spirits are supposed to be here," Tobin said. "Three guests checked in but never checked out. The most famous, of course, is Otto."

Otto Koechert (or Kocher) was in a drunken state when he arrived home at his room at the Germania house around 9:00 p.m. on March 10, 1891. The next morning, about twelve hours later, the hotel's proprietress discovered his body "stiff with death" sprawled on his bed, fully dressed.

A few days later, on March 15, Otto was the first person cremated in the newly built crematorium at Fairmount Cemetery, the first one built west of the Mississippi River. His body arrived at the crematorium on a blustery

The German American Heritage Center, built in 1862. *Courtesy Bruce Walters.*

Sunday in a horse-drawn hearse as the Davenport Band played a solemn dirge. More than 150 onlookers listened to his eulogy before his casket was "lowered smoothly and noiselessly" on a catafalque resembling a "vampire trapdoor on the theater floor" and sinking slowly downward with its burden. It is likely that his remains are still in an urn in the crematorium's storage awaiting rediscovery. More than 130 years after his death, the Germania house is now the German American Heritage Center and Museum. His obituary described him as "good natured and [he] had many friends."

However, a medium with the Whispering Souls group talked to another spirit present, asking if it would answer a question, "but he wouldn't speak to women." That didn't stop Jolene Harvey from saying something. "I blurted out a question, and he [the spirit] answered it." Jolene Harvey related, "I was told a story about how on my dad's side of the family a gentleman was brought in, and he drank too much and stepped outside, and he got hit by a horse. The medium came back and said that I was incorrect—it was the bar down the street, and it was a car. The next day, I asked mom and dad about it, and I'll be damned, that was correct information. One medium said the bartender worked here in the 1930s or '40s when it was an active bar. He felt uncomfortable with women because women weren't typically allowed in bars back then."

The Standard Hotel had modest accommodation at an affordable price. Clare Tobin said she saw an ad from the 1920s that showed rates of one dollar per night and five dollars per week.

Over the years, guests sometimes passed away at the hotel—"alcohol-related deaths," the assistant director said. "They drank too much. Some murders, suicides. A couple of fires. There was one gentleman that was so drunk he came back to his room and knocked over the oil lamp on himself and he was burnt." That man was unfortunately found by another guest and the fire department.

Clare also explained something that happened at her office:

> *On two other occasions, we had two separate paranormal groups come and do an investigation of the building. The first one was in the spring of 2023 I believe, and the second one was this past fall of 2024. Both groups made their way through the building while I was doing some work at my desk. I did not give them any information and just let them explore and see what they experienced and then spoke with them afterward to see if any of it lined up with what we know about the history of the building. An individual from both groups mentioned seeing/feeling that*

there was a middle-aged man that liked to stand behind me at my desk and "look over my shoulder" presumably looking at my computer with curiosity. Hearing this the first time was a bit startling but then hearing it a second time from a completely different group solidified this more for me. I still like to be skeptical and critical, but that one was a bit harder to explain. They assured me that it wasn't anything malicious, just pure curiosity which makes me feel a bit better about it.

Other strange occurrences that have happened at the German American Heritage Center include people detecting the smells of distinct perfume or cigar smoke when nobody is around. "The elevator door would open and then close, then open and close, open and close and then open and close with no one coming up or down," Jolene Harvey said.

WHERE: 712 WEST 2ND STREET, DAVENPORT.

Killpop

The building at 411 Persing Avenue has an interesting history, going from a brothel to soup kitchen to an art gallery.

A permit for a two-story brick building to be constructed by J.F. Nebergall for owner J. Mathews at 411 Pershing was issued by the City of Davenport on November 2, 1923. The cost was $7,500.

"When it was built, it was specifically built to be a brothel," said Philip Force, the owner of the Killpop art gallery and studio. "There are seven rooms upstairs and the madam's room was on the main floor. There were all kinds of shenanigans happening at brothels towards the Mississippi River (Bucktown). There were fighting and stabbings and such. This was meant to be a classier brothel."

It was a residential property and apartment building until about 2000, according to the City of Davenport directories.

Sister Ludmilla Benda of Father Conroy's Vineyard of Hope served its first meal on Sunday, February 19, 2006, according to Bill Wundram's column in the *Quad City Times*. Tom Roederer, owner of Bi-State Office Furniture, provided a rent-free building to Sister Ludmilla in order for them to cook and provide breakfast and lunch for 100 to 150 homeless and elderly people per week from 2006 to 2018, at which time she became ill and retired to the mother house (convent). Other volunteers kept it going until Sister

Killpop started out as a brothel and then became a soup kitchen; it's now an art gallery and studio. *Courtesy Michael McCarty.*

Ludmilla passed away. The Vineyard served its last meal in September 2019. The building was vacant until 2022, when Mr. Force opened the building as an art gallery.

Shadow figures and strange sounds have been seen and heard. "It sounds like somebody is walking down the stairs," Mr. Force said. "And you just look and there's nothing there."

There are three ghosts at the art gallery that have been seen by several people.

THE LITTLE GIRL

One witness who had seen the little girl on numerous occasions was interviewed but wished to remain anonymous. "She doesn't come down the stairs at all. She likes to dangle her feet over the edge. She is wearing a white nightgown. When she sees men, she runs away."

"She's a younger and playful spirit," said Mr. Force. "Non-threatening. She like to play with the balloon we have upstairs."

THE NUN
"A couple of people have seen a nun," Mr. Force said. (More about this later.)

THE MAN IN THE TOP HAT
"There's a top hatted shadow figure that lurks around the building but doesn't come in," Mr. Force said. "People say that they get bad a vibe from him."

MICHAEL MCCARTY'S NOTES
"The cover for my book *Dark Cities: Dark Tales* was taken across the street from the Killpop by my friend Raymond Congrove," Mr. McCarty said.

> *I first heard about this place from a friend of mine. It was around the time that it was vacant. My friend and a couple of his buddies went to a rock concert at the Adler. He parked across the street from the place.*
>
> *After the show, he and his friends went to Armored Gardens for a burger and drinks. Because my friend had to work early in the morning, he only had one beer. When he went back to his car, he had this creepy feeling that someone was watching him. He turned around and saw a nun on the second floor looking down at him, and then she disappeared.*

Mr. McCarty commented about the interview with Mr. Force:

> *I was interviewing Philip Force and a friend of his on the main floor of Killpop. Maybe ten minutes into the interview I heard a loud knock coming from above. I said to Philip and the friend, "Did you hear that?" And they said yes.*
>
> *Maybe five minutes later, the same knock. After the interview I went up to all seven rooms to see if anyone was there and there was no one. I did the same thing in the basement.*
>
> *I went into the first room off the stairs and put the balloon in the corner and secured it. I went downstairs and came back up. Five minutes later, the balloon had moved about five feet. I was talking to Philip at the time in the hallway next to the room and I could see the balloon was moving on the floor, although there was no draft or breeze in the windowless room.*
>
> *I came back upstairs five minutes later, and the balloon had not moved at all. I think the spirit knew we were aware of its presence.*

WHERE: 411 PERSHING AVENUE, DAVENPORT.

Haunted Jails

Squirrel Cage Jail

The Squirrel Cage Jail in Council Bluffs has an awfully playful name for such a terrifying nightmare of a structure built in 1885. At its center is a three-story cylinder of thirty jail cells that rotate as a single unit when cranked by hand by the warden. Broken arms and legs were routine for prisoners who stuck their limbs through their cell bars as the cage turned. The rotary mechanism was disabled in 1960 after a prisoner died and a malfunction prevented the retrieval of his corpse for two days.

To one side of the rotating cage is a harrowing hallway that ends in a solitary confinement cell. The cell is approximately one by two feet in width and length, allowing a man to stand in a coffin-sized space behind a heavy jail door. One prisoner was held there for ten days. The jail also held children as young as three in juvenile detention. Minor thieves were housed with murderers. One man was jailed for writing a $1.50 check that bounced; Jake Bird murdered dozens with an axe.

In 1928, Jake Bird was a twenty-four-year-old transient railroad worker when he broke into a home in Iowa, attacking the couple living there with an axe. Bird served a half year in the Squirrel Cage Jail before being transferred to the Iowa State Penitentiary for twelve years.

In 1947, he was arrested for the brutal slaying of Bertha Kludt and her daughter in Tacoma, Washington. After his guilty verdict was read, Bird spoke passionately for twenty minutes, ending with a declaration, "All you guys who had anything to do with this case are going to die before I do," according to the *Seattle Times*.

Jake Bird's mug shot. *From washingtonstatepenitentiary.com.*

While Bird's execution was delayed, five men connected with Bird's trial died suddenly, including the judge, Edward Hodge; Sherman Lyons, the police detective who interrogated Bird; and James Selden, his defense attorney.

His execution was delayed for a year and a half while officers investigated the additional forty-four murders he confessed to. His victims included three people—including an eight-year-old child—in Omaha, just across the Missouri River from Council Bluffs.

Behind the bars at the Squirrel Cage Jail. *Courtesy Bruce Walters.*

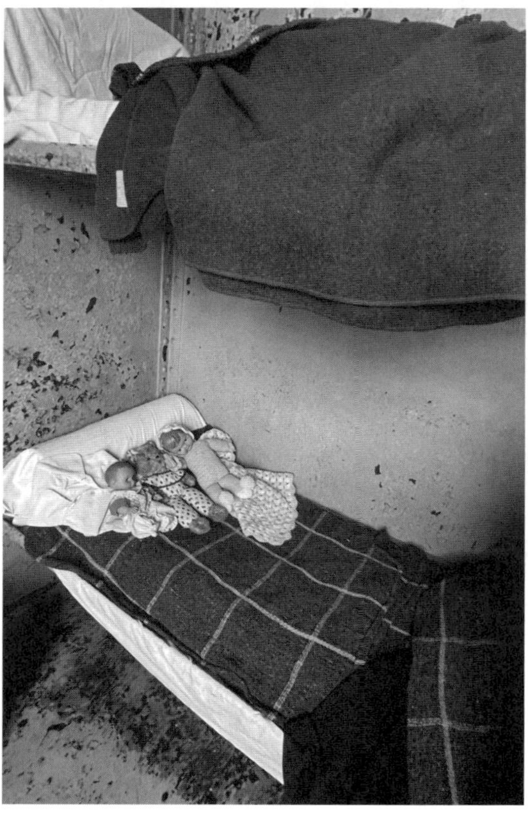

Above: A view from the top at the Squirrel Cage Jail. *Courtesy Bruce Walters.*

Left: One of the cells at Squirrel Cage Jail. The dolls were for the children who stayed there, some as young as five years old. *Courtesy Bruce Walters.*

Above: Anamosa State Penitentiary. *Courtesy Bruce Walters.*

Right: Boot Hill Cemetery, Anamosa State Penitentiary Cemetery. *Courtesy Bruce Walters.*

The Squirrel Cage Jail was declared unfit for human habitation in 1969. Its inmates were removed to other prisons. It is now open for tours, paranormal investigations and overnight fundraiser lock-ins. If you visit it, don't say you weren't warned. It is eerie. Very eerie.

Where: 226 Pearl Street, Council Bluffs.

Rockwell City, North Central Correctional Facility Rockwell City

Originally a female reformatory constructed from 1916 to 1918 by the inmates incarnated there, the building was called the "cottage," and there was no fence on the premises. The oldest building used to be a hospital. Sights of a female figure walking on the lower levers have been seen. Loud screams and doors opening and closing by themselves have been reported. There is a graveyard at NCCF that has female inmates and their babies buried there. In 1982, it became a men's medium-security prison, and they installed a twelve-foot fence.

Where: 313 Landale, Rockwell City.

Mount Pleasant, Iowa Medium-Security Prison

The Mount Pleasant Mental Institute, the first mental hospital in the state, is located on 152 acres (roughly the size of 115 football fields). It opened in 1861 as Iowa's Lunatic Asylum. In 1976, it became an Iowa men's reformatory, a medium-security prison. In 2016, it was reclassified as a minimum-security facility. Apparitions have been seen wandering the halls at night. Loud furniture has been heard being dragged across empty cells.

Where: 1200 East Washington Street, Mount Pleasant.

Historic Iowa State Penitentiary

The maximum-security prison was established in 1839 one year after Iowa became a territory (seven years before Iowa's statehood). After 178 years, it

The noose used to hang Charles Noel Brown, the last man hanged in Iowa, on July 24, 1962, on display at the Squirrel Cage Jail, Council Bluffs. *Courtesy Bruce Walters.*

closed its doors in 2015 and was reopened two miles south of the original prison. The penitentiary was intended to house only offenders who were thirty-one years or older or those convicted of the most serious of crimes.

When it was open, Iowa state prison guards refused to go to the end of a certain corridor at night. Inmates experienced cold spots and unexplained noise of chairs clanking after sunset. Inmates have been choked by unseen forces alone in their locked cells.

The prison still gives tours.

WHERE: NO. 3 JOHN BENNETT DRIVE, FORT MADISON.

John Looney and Others

Daniel Drost (1861–1939)

Rock Island, that Citadel of Sin, is the wickedest city in the United States of America, bar none. And the leader of that wickedness is John Patrick Looney.

—*evangelist Billy Sunday*

On October 6, 1922, hundreds of baseball fans gathered around a scoreboard in the front window of the *Argus* in downtown Rock Island to follow the third game of the World Series.

Halfway through the game, two large black cars pulled to a stop in the middle of the street. Exiting their cars, several men stood in the street to fire guns at two men, who returned their fire. The fans scrambled away from the ricocheting bullets in panic. Several men were shot.

The gunmen had targeted John Looney, Rock Island's infamous gangster. As he recounted, "They all seemed to be firing at me. I saw they had a shotgun and a rifle. They all wanted to kill me." He survived, but his twenty-one-year-old son, Connor, was shot dead.

John Looney controlled a criminal organization that extended far beyond the community through extortion, corruption, bombings and murder. As Roger Ruthhart wrote for the *Argus*, "A federal investigation revealed that 170 or more illegal businesses had been paying for protection from Mr. Looney." Eight murders and numerous shootings were attributed to him and his men.

However, one of Looney's most loyal lieutenants, Dan Drost, was one of the gunmen who had tried to kill him in that October 6 gun battle. Drost had served as the editor of the *Rock Island News*, a scandal sheet Looney had created to intimidate and blackmail his enemies. He served a year in prison for a libelous story published in the paper in 1921. Upon his release, Drost tried to collect money in compensation from Looney. Instead, he was cheated of his life savings, leaving him penniless. He was in his sixties.

Drost was again sentenced to prison, this time for his role in the ambush that resulted in Connor Looney's death. After serving eight and a half years in the Illinois State Penitentiary in Joliet, he returned to live in downtown Rock Island on an old-age retirement grant and from income he received from menial duties at the rooming house where he lived.

Davenport's newspaper, the *Daily Times*, characterized Drost as "the man of mystery of the once notorious Looney gang" when it reported his death in 1939. He was also a man of contradictions. Although he served as the editor of Looney's newspaper, he contended that he could neither read nor write. Though loyal, he kept John Looney's eldest daughter, Kathleen, from the gangster's influence by paying for her to move to a convent in St. Louis. Looney would never forgive him for this. He married, but his wife discovered that he had married her under a false name: Daniel Chandler. She divorced him.

Daniel Drost is buried at Chippiannock Cemetery in Rock Island (North Public, lot 22, grave 6), not far from the unmarked grave of Connor Looney, the young man he was convicted of killing. The grave of this "man of mystery" is also unmarked.

WHERE: CHIPPIANNOCK CEMETERY, 2901 12TH STREET, ROCK ISLAND, ILLINOIS.

John Connor Looney (1901–1922), aka "Crazy Connie"

Road to Perdition was originally a graphic novel written by Max Allan Collins, with artwork by Richard Piers Paryner. It was then turned into a movie starring Academy Award winners Paul Newman as John Rooney and Daniel Craig as his son, Connor Rooney. The graphic novel and movie were based on gangster John Looney, with the last name being changed for the movie.

For the book *Esoteria-Land* by Michael McCarty, Max Allan Collins was interviewed about the graphic novel and movie changes:

> Road to Perdition *was shown by my literary agent to a Hollywood agent, who was smart enough to see the father-and-son connection and submitted it to Richard and Dean Zanuck, a father-and-son producing team. Richard Zanuck, one of the true surviving greats in business, showed it to Steven Spielberg who loved the graphic novel, and, of course, everything else fell into place.*
>
> *I have no problem with any of the changes in the movie. It's a great film and will be watched and discussed if movies are watched and discussed. Our graphic novel stands on its own and benefits from this wonderful treatment. Some changes made by Sam Mendes and David Self, director and screenwriter respectively, are improvements, others are not; but each is its own work, and I believe both will stand the test of time.*

> *The Looney change is ironic, and relates to the graphic novel source material—Hollywood found the name too "comic booky," not understanding its reality. Earlier cuts of the movie included more Quad-Cities identifiers—the opening at one time had a superimposed "Rock Island, Illinois, 1931." The scene in which Hanks kills the gangster at the gambling joint/whorehouse/nightclub is in Davenport, Iowa* [the Government Bridge is in the background of the establishing shot].

John Connor Looney was the youngest of three children by John Looney and Nora O'Connor Looney. They also had two daughters: Kathleen Looney (1894–1942) and Ursula Mary Looney (1897–1984).

Nora O'Connor passed away in 1903 from cancer. Young Connor was three. After his wife's death, John's crime went from petty to more serious and deadly. Kathleen became a nun, and Ursula married New Mexico rancher Frank Leslie Hamblin. Unfortunately, Connor followed in his father's footsteps.

In *Ghosts of the Quad Cities*, Bucktown in downtown Davenport, Iowa, was called the "Wickedest Town in America." In *Early Days in Davenport and Rock Island*, Nick Vulich referred to that, saying, "If that's true, Rock Island missed it by a nosebleed." Rock Island had more than 150 saloons, brothels and gambling houses.

Irish gangster John Looney had businesses pay protection money. Rock Island saloon owner William Gamble decided to stop paying after watching a prostitute being beaten death with a beer bottle in Helen Van Dale's resort by Police Chief Thomas Cox. Word on the street was that Gamble had turned over canceled checks for Looney's protection to the feds.

On July 31, 1922, Gamble was gunned down. Two cars were involved, one with John Looney and driver Lawrence Pedigo and the other with his son driving. This was one murder too many for the Irish gangster, as it began a gang war and led to John Looney's downfall.

On October 6, John and Connor were ambushed in front of the Sherman Hotel in Rock Island. As everyone got out of their car, John could see that trouble was coming. "Come on son, they got us," he shouted, but it was too late. Connor sidestepped and then reached for his weapon, while his father and others slipped into the hotel. Connor received five steel-jacketed revolver bullets and one hundred buckshots. Looney held his dying son, whose last words were, "My gun jammed."

Anthony Billburg and others were charged with the murder of Connor. Billburg, a wealthy saloon owner and one-time friend of Looney turned bitter enemy, hired Clarence Darrow to defend him for the sum of $30,000. Still, he received a thirty-year sentence.

John Connor Looney was buried in an unmarked grave at Calvary Cemetery in Rock Island not too far from Dan Durst's final resting spot at Chippiannock Cemetery.

WHERE: CALVARY CEMETERY, 2901 12TH STREET, ROCK ISLAND, ILLINOIS.

Helen Van Dale (1895–1951), aka "Queen of the Looney Underworld"

All heads turned as Helen Van Dale, the notorious "Queen of the Looney Underworld," walked to the witness stand in the trial of Rock Island's mayor, police chief and one of John Looney's henchmen. The charges included graft, illicit gambling and alcohol sale during Prohibition.

According to *The Citadel of Sin*, "The women whispered and pulled their jackets tightly closed; men, who had come to court dressed in suits, acted like little boys, and pointed and elbowed each other."

Van Dale was released from jail before the trial after she agreed to testify. When she stepped to the witness stand, she was dressed in a mink cape, a black hat and a satin dress with a lace collar and wore gloves. She admitted to running a brothel and that she was involved in Looney's liquor trade through the Rock Island police chief.

Two years later, she testified in trials against John Looney, who faced charges ranging from murder to conspiracy. In one exchange, Van Dale testified that she had threatened to kill Looney if he tried to blackmail her. She stated that Looney "said he couldn't be killed, that the devil protected him."

John Looney was found guilty on all counts and was sentenced to fifteen to twenty-one years in prison. Van Dale had been charged with the same crimes, but they were dropped.

The trials ended Looney's criminal empire, which had plagued Rock Island and Davenport's Bucktown for a generation. At the time of his incarceration, Looney's wealth was estimated to be in excess of $20 million in today's money.

Short documentary edited by five-time Emmy winner Kelly Rundle and created by Bruce Walters. It was shown on October 6, 2024, at the Putnam's screening of *Road to Perdition* in Davenport. *Courtesy Bruce Walters.*

Looney and his henchmen were now in prison, and Looney's son had been murdered. Rock Island detective Charles Ginnane had committed suicide. Police Chief Tom Cox died of a heart attack or syphilis (depending on which newspaper you read). And Helen's younger sister, Dimples, took her own life. She was just twenty-four.

Helen Van Dale was born Eula Elizabeth Lee in 1893 in Paris City, Illinois, near the Indiana border. She came to the Tri-Cities (now Quad Cities) in 1914, followed by her mother and sister, who assisted her in running several "disorderly houses" in Davenport. In time, she ran some 150 of these disorderly houses, creating a prostitution empire that reached into surroundings states.

She ran afoul of the law repeatedly. But the charges became more serious when William Gamble, who ran a "soft drink establishment," a cover for illegal activities, was gunned down in downtown Rock Island in 1922. His establishment was adjacent to one of Van Dale's brothels.

The unmarked grave site of Helen Van Dale. She was buried between her fourth and fifth husbands. *Courtesy Bruce Walters.*

Gamble had seen Rock Island Police Chief Tom Cox beat one of Van Dale's prostitutes to death after she had quarreled with Van Dale. It was the last straw for Gamble, and he began to meet with federal officers. He had just left a secret meeting with them when he was silenced. Seven federal Prohibition agents were immediately assigned to start an investigation into his death.

Van Dale was one of the people charged with his murder. She was jailed also for illegal gambling and prostitution and for violating the Mann Act (the "White Slavery Law"). And *this* is where our story began, with Helen walking to the witness stand.

Helen Van Dale disappeared from the public eye shortly after Looney's conviction. She died at the age of fifty-eight in 1951. She is buried alongside her mother and between the graves of her fourth and fifth husbands at Fairmount Cemetery in Davenport. Her grave, mysteriously, is unmarked (GVA, lot 217, grave 7). Helen owned land, a nightclub and a taxi service at the time of her death, so the decision not to install a gravestone was not because of financial reasons.

WHERE: FAIRMOUNT CEMETERY, 3902 ROCKINGHAM ROAD, DAVENPORT.

Ghosts

JOHN CONNOR LOONEY

Peg Rounds, the museum curator at the Hauberg Estates and cofounder and paranormal investigator of Whispering Souls Paranormal, had an encounter with John Connor Looney's spirit:

> *The first time I encountered Connor, I was doing the tour that night* [in downtown Rock Island] *and he came up behind me, and I tasted blood, tasted iron. And another tour guide who was with me that night saw him coming too, and she stepped behind me.*
>
> *He was quiet that night. From then on, he would stand there, and he would say "hi." When the other another medium would do the tours, Connor would ask him "Where's Peg?"*
>
> *Connor would often tell me that he was drug into the family business. He told me about the day he was killed. He said that he didn't know where they came from. He would often say he was innocent. He wasn't guilty, like everybody makes him out to be.*
>
> *If you go in looking for the dark in people, you're going to find it in everybody. If you go in looking for the light in people, that's what you will find. I look for the light. The light side of Connor was him being just a person and doing what his family told him to.*

HELEN VAN DALE'S PALMER INN

On December 5, 1922, Helen Van Dale was arrested at her Palmer Inn on Nahant Road on charges of violating the White Slavery Law by taking a sixteen-year-old Iowa girl to Illinois.

Bruce Walters and a local historian were doing research on where the Palmer Inn might be now. The roads and that section of Davenport have changed a lot over the last century (Nahant, then New Rockingham, then Davenport).

Mr. Walters used a map from 1919 from the *Atlas of Iowa* and then included plans for the development of "New Rockingham" at the corner of Wapello Road and South Concord, which runs along a mysterious swamp-like shore of the Mississippi River. The map speculatively identified two hotels as the Palmer Inn and Hollywood Inn.

Nahant Road and the most likely location for the Palmer Inn would be at the intersection of South Concord and Wapello Roads. On one side of the road, there is an auto scrape yard; the other is marshlands and

The location of the Palmer Inn on Wapello Avenue, near South Concord. *Courtesy Bruce Walters.*

wilderness. The historian said that some of the foundations of the Palmer Inn are on the metal scrape yard side. Mr. Walters had a hunch that it was on the other side.

To determine the destination site of Palmer Inn, we contacted medium Peg Rounds and took her to the area. This is what she said:

> *There's someone screaming. She's terrified. She's on that side of the road* [pointing to the marshland side]. *There's a driveway up there* [pointing to the landfill side]. *White house with green shutters. There are a lot of people coming in and going out. There's music. There's like parties. You smell alcohol. The girls that worked there were really scared. Some of them have bruises. There was a dirt road, cars driving up gathered dust.*
>
> *There's somebody important there. But they're real quiet about who it is. There's a room that they're in, nobody goes into and there's somebody standing outside the door, very secretive. Pretty fancy place. There is a staircase that goes up to another floor, people constantly walking up and down it. There's just a feeling of terror around it.*
>
> *There are two guys talking. And one guy asks, "What did you tell your boss?" And the other guy laughs. "I had some errands to run." And he laughs. There's the presence of a female. She isn't like the others. I'm not sure if it's Helen or not. Her hair's up in a bun. She dresses differently than the other girls. "Quiet. Somebody's coming up." Now they're screaming, a lot of screaming. There's a guy, he smells of alcohol and cigars. He terrifies the girls.*

After that, she saw a farmer, and he said his name was Jackson. He was wearing overalls and grinning. He didn't say much after that. She also saw a large Indigenous tribe on the marshland side going about their daily business. "There's a lot of energy here," Peg said. "I keep seeing a shadow moving down in those trees. Deep down."

Here are Michael McCarty's observations: "It was a semi-warm fall afternoon. Peg, her husband, Kevin, and son, Josh, meet me at the Nahant Marsh Education Center, which is nearby, and I drive them to the intersection of Walpello and South Concord and park. We got out of my car and walked down the road. The whole time it is a calm, lovely afternoon. The moment Peg starts to talk, there is a slight breeze, and the longer she talks, the breeze becomes brisker. And when she finishes, the breeze finished. Very eerie."

Part III
A LITTLE EERIE

Iowa's TV Horror Hosts

Gravesend Manor was on WOI-TV Channel 5 in Des Moines. Ed Weiss hosted from the 1950s and early 1960s. Mr. Weiss played Malcom, the butler. Ron Scott originally cohosted as Claude the Great. They were later joined by Claude's brother, Clyde (actor unknown). Also on the show was Jim Varnum, who played the Duke of Desmodas, and John Voight, who played Esmeralda.

Chiller Thriller was on WQAD Channel 8 in the Quad Cities. Gene Edwards played Dr. Igor in the 1960s.

Acri Creature Feature was on WQAD Channel 8 in the Quad Cities. It ran from 1969 until 1976, with revival seasons in 1982 and 2003. It was hosted by Chuck Acri, who owned a local siding company. Ken Gibson played Vincent Hedges, the vampire (his name was a play on a popular cigarette at the time); Ken Williams played Beauregard, the werewolf; George Sedlack played the Missing Link, a caveman; Wilda McMillion played Bertie, the maid; and Don Molander played Emmit, the hunchback.

Saturday Nightmare was on KCRG Channel 9 in Cedar Rapids. Bruce F. Gantenbein hosted from 1986 to 1988. Mr. Gantenbein played Dr. Morbius.

Another revival of *Acri Creature Feature* ran without Chuck Acri from 2005 to 2007. Scott Naumann played Count Olaf D Graves, Jim Seward played the count's buddy, Max Moiderer. Barb Enstrom played Hot Toddie, Jamie Em Johnson played Esmerelda Jonis, Margo McInnis played Veiny and Stephanie Seward played Goth Girl.

On the set of *Midnight Mausoleum*, with hostess Marlena Midnite. *Courtesy Michael McCarty.*

Midnite Mausoleum was on WQAD Channel 8 and WQAD MyTV 8.3 Quad Cities. It was hosted by Aude Metzger as Marlena Midnite and cohosted by Robyn Graves. After Ms. Graves left the show, there were two cohosts, Jennifer Boisen as Elizadeath and Cat Ziggy as herself. The show debuted in 2009 and is still running today. Other characters include Andrew Smith, playing the voice of Dr. Thaddeus Bones, a talking skeleton; Franklyn, a Frankenstein finger puppet; and the adorable Wolfred, a fury werewolf hand puppet. Blake Powell is the director of the show. In 2019, Aude Metzer and company were inducted into the Official Horror Host of Fame.

IOWA'S CONSERVATIONIST AND THE DEVIL'S TOWER CONNECTION

Before *Silent Spring* by Rachel Carson...before Ding Darling...before President Teddy Roosevelt...before the Devil's Tower and *Close Encounters of the Third Kind*...there was Major John F. Lacey.

There is plaque at Lacey State Park, in the southern part of the state in Keosauqua, Iowa, dedicated to Lacey, who sponsored America's first federal conservation act. Just one of the federal laws he sponsored, the Antiquities Act of 1906, was "intended to save the prehistoric Indian ruins of the Southwest," but more than two hundred national monuments, including many large, scenic parklands, have been established.

President Theodore Roosevelt declared Devils Tower in Wyoming as the first national monument on September 24, 1906. Effigy Mounds National Monument, Iowa's only "national park," was established by Harry Truman on October 25, 1949, under the provisions of this act.

WHERE: LACEY-KEOSAUQUA STATE PARK, 22895 LACEY TRAIL, KEOSAUQUA, IOWA 52565.

Stony Hollow Cliff

One of the most famous roads in Burlington is Snake Alley. Lombard Street in San Francisco is known for its winding path, but North 6th Road (nicknamed Snake Alley) has sharper curves. It was built to help connect Burlington's bluff to Heritage Hill's commercial district below. The five half curves and two quarter curves make it a perilous and steep path. Robert L. Ripley deemed it "the crookedest street in the world" and designated it *Ripley's Believe It or Not!*'s no. 1 Odd Spot in its "Odd Spots Across America" campaign.

Also in Burlington, but not as famous, there's one of the most haunted roads in Iowa, Stony Hollow Road. Traveling down this short, rural roadway, you can see a cliff towering over the asphalt. This is the spot of the road ghost, Lucinda. According to legend, she was waiting on the side of the road for her husband, but he was terribly late. Assuming the worst, Lucinda thought that he had run off with another woman, climbed to the top of the cliff and jumped to her death. Her husband showed up to find his bride dead.

The ghost of Lucinda still haunts the area today. After dark, shout her name three times and the faint ghostly bride may appear near the top of the cliff. If she puts a rose by someone's feet, they will die the next day. She is said to be a shy apparition and is easily scared off.

Where: Stony Hollow Road, Burlington.

Cresco Opera House

The Cresco Opera House, also known as the Cresco Theatre, is a historic building that opened in 1915 and is still operating today. For more than a century, the theater has had movies (from the silent era to the "talkies" to 3D to Dolby Surround Sound to digital projection), vaudeville, actors, musicians, opera singers, community theater productions and, of course, ghosts.

Spectral vaudeville performers have been seen on the stage. There are reports of someone sitting in the audience during practice and disappearing when approached.

One former concession worker said to the *Cresco Times*, "I worked at the Cresco Theatre for over a year when I was in high school. For over three months, none of us would work alone. We would see feet walking behind the screen, doors would open and close on their own."

In the basement, there have been strange electrical disturbances, odd sounds and unknown voices when the place is empty.

WHERE: 115 2ND AVENUE WEST, CRESCO.

THE FUTURE HOME OF CAPTAIN KIRK

The small town of Riverside sits between a big gambling casino and an Amish community. Horse-drawn carriages can be seen crossing through town. But what puts this place on the eerie map is neither of those things.

In a city council meeting in March 1985, council member Steve Miller made a motion to claim that Riverside, Iowa, was—or would be—the birthplace of *Star Trek*'s Captain James Kirk. The council voted unanimously to support his out-of-this-world proposal.

Miller's inspiration came from the pages of *The Making of Star Trek* by Gene Roddenberry. There he wrote that Kirk was born in a small town in Iowa. Riverside, a quiet town of 826 in 1985, fit the description. The town embraced its newfound identity, changing its slogan from "Where the Best Begins" to "Where the Trek Begins."

Wikipedia's biography on the fictional character reports, "James Tiberius Kirk was born in Riverside, Iowa, on March 22, 2233, where he was raised by his parents, George and Winona Kirk." It is now canon! March 22, 1931, is William Shatner's actual birthday, although it's 302 years in the future (March 22, 2233) for the captain of the USS *Enterprise*.

The Voyage Home, Riverside History Museum, opened in 2008. It is located at 361 East 1st Street on a bend on Highway 22. Across the street, a bronze sculpture of Captain Kirk, dedicated in 2018, gazes skyward. His eyes are alight with distant wonder. Yet beneath the heroic visage, there lingers an unsettling truth: Kirk's face has a dark side.

William Shatner's features, immortalized as Kirk, found a second life as something far more sinister. Hollywood repurposed his likeness, stripping away the color and softening the lines until what remained was pallid, blank and eerily emotionless. That mask, worn by Michael Myers in *Halloween*,

Captain Kirk statue and Michael Myers mask side by side. *Photos by Bruce Walters.*

became a face of terror. Michael McCarty interviewed director and screenwriter John Carpenter for his book *Modern Mythmakers: 35 Interviews with Horror and Science Fiction Writers and Filmmakers* and is a big fan of the film.

In the documentary *Halloween: 25 Years of Terror*, Tommy Lee Wallace (the production designer and co-editor of the film with Charles Bornstein) said that John Carpenter and Debra Hill (producer and co-writer) bought different Halloween masks to test. Wallace bought a familiar clown mask, which was used for young Michael when he kills his older sister Judith (former *Playboy* model Sandy Johnson in the film). Wallace, of course, found a Don Post Studios *Star Trek* mask of Captain Kirk (it is rumored to have cost only two dollars). He painted it white, widened the eye holes a bit and colored and teased the hair. Carpenter and Hill picked the Captain Kirk mask for their Michael Myers character to wear in the movie.

As Rick Sternbach—an illustrator/designer on *Star Trek: The Motion Picture*, *The Next Generation*, *Deep Space Nine*, *Voyager* and *Nemesis*—once posted on his Facebook page:

> *I was hired as an illustrator on* Halloween 2 *in 1981, working for production designer J. Michael Riva. In a supply cabinet at Pumpkin Pie Productions, we had one mask left from the original* Halloween *and no idea where to get any others for the sequel.*

> *It appeared that we'd need to go check out some of the toy stores and such, but I noticed that there was some wording molded into the neck area. There was a model number and "Don Post Studios." I made a call, read off the model number, and the word came back. "It's our Captain Kirk mask." I asked if we could buy a number of them, and was told, "We'll give you a box. Just give us credit." With that, I turned the official dealings over to the higher-ups. Brush with greatness.*

And so, in Riverside, Captain Kirk's bronze form stands watch night and day. His upward gaze inspires dreams of exploration. But what if that mask of a face—suddenly pallid and blank—turns to stare at you?

Where: 361 East 1st Street, Riverside.

AFTERWORD

Aloha! It is a greeting in Hawaiian that means hello and goodbye, much like *salut* in French or *ciao* in Italian. Here it means goodbye as we prepare to leave the pages of *Eerie Iowa*. But before we leave, let's talk about the authors, Michael and Bruce, and the book one last time.

A little over a year ago, I got a Facebook message from a local gentleman named Michael McCarty. Michael introduced himself and explained that he had sent me a friend request due to the fact that he was contemplating writing a book on a subject very near and dear to my heart. I quickly added him as a friend and wished him luck with his project.

Soon after that, Michael said he had a question for me. I was quite intrigued and felt the best way for him to ask the question was in person, so I invited Michael and his wife, Cindy, to my home for a glass of wine. Michael explained that their schedules were extremely tight but that they could spare forty-five minutes on a Thursday for a quick drink.

I looked forward to the evening and was all prepared, I thought, for a brief introduction, a speedy glass of wine and a swift question. Actually, I got a delightful overview of Michael's life as an award-winning author, an in-depth look at the adorable relationship he has with his beautiful wife and the ability to go through three bottles of wine while being asked if there was a possibility I would be willing to collaborate on future projects. My answer was a resounding yes!

Let's talk a little about the other half of this book, Bruce Walters. He is a Professor Emeritus at Western Illinois University. Just writing those words down sounds impressive, and they are. He was a teacher for more than three decades, and as a teacher for two decades myself, I understand what a grand service to the young minds of Iowa and Illinois he performed.

Michael McCarty and Veronique Fernandez at the Swinging Bridge of Columbus Junction. Veronique smiles at the camera as Michael holds on for dear life. *Courtesy Veronique Fernandez.*

Besides being a retired teacher, Bruce is a writer and lecturer at many events in the Quad Cities. He wrote for the *River Cities Reader*, including such columns as "Buried Stories" and "Art in Plain Sight," and held interviews with the likes of Tobias Forge from the Swedish rock band Ghost and 1960s singer-songwriter and guitarist Donovan. Mostly I was aware of Bruce's art and photography, but let's continue about that night with the McCartys a year ago.

To say I was impressed by the McCartys is a true understatement. Talking to Michael is like talking to a who's who of horror. He is part historian, part storyteller and part animator in how he brings the creepy to life. You cannot come up with a horror question that Michael does not have the answer to or a horror author or celebrity that Michael hasn't interviewed, which is why I was overjoyed when I found out that my husband and I had been to a few eerie locations that Michael had not yet visited. Naturally, we offered to take Michael and Cindy to Hickory Hill Cemetery in Charlotte, Iowa, and I'm happy to write that it was great day; you learned about the trip in this book.

I have not yet met Bruce, but hopefully I will do so in the near future. I have seen his photography, art and writing in *Eerie Iowa*, and I am very impressed. He can capture both the beauty and eeriness of a location in one photograph. If the photos don't give you goosebumps, Bruce's artwork certainly will. His art has the ability to stay with you, like the flavor of a fine wine, even after you have set the book down. That, to me, is the true test of a real artist.

I'm so excited that I was able to be a small part of this book. I'm also very excited to think that I'm just beginning my relationship with Michael and that there will be many more adventures to come. If I may give you a bit of advice: grab this book and keep it relatively handy. When you are out on

Bruce Walters and the statue of Captain Kirk in Riverside. *Courtesy Al Bieg.*

the roads in the Quad Cities and have a little extra time, flip to a chapter and do a little detour. Drive to one of these locations that the authors so carefully researched and wrote about. Hop out of your car and take a little stroll. What did you think? What did you feel? What did you see? You may not have run into Bigfoot or a ghost, but I guarantee you will have your own story to share. If you share this story with someone you've just met, you may find yourself with a brand-new lifelong friend, just like me! *Salut*!

—VERONIQUE FERNANDEZ

BIBLIOGRAPHY

General Use Sources

Bannister, Megan. *Secret Iowa: A Guide to the Weird, Wonderful and Obscure*. Reedy Press, 2023.

Brassard, John, and John Brassard Jr. *Scott County Cemeteries* (Images of America series). Arcadia Publishing, 2011.

Clark, Jerome. *Unexplained!: 347 Strange Sightings, Incredible Occurrences and Puzzling Physical Phenomena*. Visible Ink Press, 1993.

Freeburg, Jessica, and Natalie Fowler. *Monsters of the Midwest: True Tales of Bigfoot, Werewolves and Other Legendary Creatures*. Adventure Publications, 2016.

Grimes, Bret. *The St. Elizabeth's Hospital Fire in Iowa.* The History Press, 2024.

Hammer, Richard, and Roger Ruthhart. *Citadel of Sin: The John Looney Story*. Moline Dispatch Publishing Company, 2007.

Hauck, Dennis William. *Haunted Places: The National Directory: Ghostly Abodes, Sacred Sites, UFO Landings and Other Supernatural Locations*. Penguin, 1994.

Lewis, Chad, and Terry Fisk. *Iowa Road Guide to Haunted Locations*. Unexplained Research Publishing Company, 2007.

Lewis, Chad, Kevin Lee Nelson and Noah Voss. *The Van Meter Visitor: A True and Mysterious Encounter with the Unknown*. On the Road Publications, 2013.

McCarty, Michael. *Esoteria-Land*. BearManor Media, 2009.

McCarty, Michael, and Connie Corcoran Wilson. *Ghostly Tales of Route 66*. Quixote Press, 2008.

McCarty, Michael, and John Brassard Jr. *Eerie Quad Cities*. The History Press, 2021.

McCarty, Michael, and Kristin DeMarr. *Quad Cities Beer: A History*. The History Press, 2023.

McCarty, Michael, and Mark McLaughlin. *Ghosts of the Quad Cities.* The History Press, 2019.

Nielson, Chris. *Fear and Fascination in Edinburgh Manor*. Independently published, 2023.

Partsch, Tammy. *It Happened in Iowa*. Twodot, 2017.

Powell-Douglass, Minda. *Chippiannock Cemetery*. Images of America series. Arcadia Publishing, 2007.

Scott, Beth, and Michael Norman. *Haunted Heartland*. Dorset Press, 1985.

Smith, Doug. *Davenport*. Postcard History series. Arcadia Publishing, 2007.

Steiger, Brad. *Real Ghosts, Restless Spirits and Haunted Places*. Visible Ink Press, 2003.

Trollinger, Vernon. *Haunted Iowa City*. The History Press, 2011.

Vulich, Nick. *Early Days in Davenport and Rock Island*. Lulu, 2021.

———. *Gruesome Iowa: Murder, Madness and the Macabre in the Hawkeye State*. Lulu, 2019.

———. *Gruesome Quad-Cities: Murder, Madness and the Macabre Along the Mississippi*. Lulu, 2020.

Weatherly, David. *Monsters of the Hawkeye State: Cryptids & Legends of Iowa (Monsters of America)*. Eerie Lights, 2022.

PREFACE

Bannister, Megan. *Secret Iowa: A Guide to the Weird, Wonderful and Obscure*. Reedy Press, 2023.

Brilliant Maps. "Percentage of Each US State Occupied by Corn Fields." https://brilliantmaps.com.

eReference Desk. "Iowa History Timeline." ereferencedesk.com.

Hoyt, Alia. "Why Do Liminal Spaces Feel So Unsettling, Yet So Familiar?" Medium. medium.com.

Iowa State University. https://www.iastate.edu.

Medium. "The Psychology of Liminal Spaces, On the Transitional Zones Between 'What Was' and 'What's Next.'" medium.com.

Mott, David C. "Index to Abandoned Towns in Iowa." *Annals of Iowa* 18, no. 3 (1932): 189–220. https://doi.org/10.17077/0003-4827.5529.

NASA. "What Are the Van Allen Belts and Why Do They Matter?" https://science.nasa.gov.

On This Day. "Early Iowa History." onthisday.com.

———. "Iowa History Timeline." onthisday.com.

Partsch, Tammy. *It Happened in Iowa*. Twodot, 2017.

Pine Barrens Institute. "Cryptid Profile: The South River Monster Battle of 1884." https://pinebarrensinstitute.com.

Travel Iowa. "Lewis & Clark National Historic Trail." traveliowa.com.

Wikipedia. "Van Allen Radiation Belt." wikipedia.com.

Curious Creatures, UFOs and Strange Happenings

The Van Meter Visitor

Armstrong, Perry. *The Piasa, or The Devil Among the Indians*. E.B. Fletcher, Book and Job Printer, 1887.

Bannister, Megan. *Secret Iowa: A Guide to the Weird, Wonderful and Obscure*. Reedy Press, 2023.

Des Moines Daily News. "Town of Van Meter Wrought Up Over a Fishy Story: Hideous Monster Alleged to Have Terrified All." October 4, 1903.

Freeburg, Jessica, and Natalie Fowler. *Monsters of the Midwest: True Tales of Bigfoot, Werewolves and Other Legendary Creatures*. Adventure Publications, 2016.

Lewis, Chad. Interview by Michael McCarty, June 2024.

Lewis, Chad, Kevin Lee Nelson and Noah Voss. *The Van Meter Visitor: A True and Mysterious Encounter with the Unknown*. On the Road Publications, 2013.

New York World. "This Monster Like a Maniac's Dream: Awful Winged for Shedding Dazzling Light Terrifies an Iowa Town." October 5, 1903.

St. Paul Globe. "A Winged Monster Creature Emitting a Dazzling Light Terrifies Hawkeyes." October 1903.

Vulich, Nick. *Gruesome Iowa: Murder, Madness and the Macabre in the Hawkeye State*. Lulu, 2019.

Weatherly, David. *Monsters of the Hawkeye State: Cryptids & Legends of Iowa (Monsters of America)*. Eerie Lights, 2022.

Dogman of Cedar Rapids

Brittanica. "Dire Wolf." britannica.com.

Finn, Neoma. Interview by Michael McCarty, August 2024.

Bigfoot in Iowa

Bigfoot Field Researchers Organization (BFRO). "Reports for Iowa." https://www.bfro.net.

Finn, Neoma. Interview by Michael McCarty, August 2024.

Henderson, Frank. *Bigfoot in Iowa*. Independently published, 2023.

Liegois, Madelin. "Searching for Bigfoot in Iowa: A Group of Iowa Based Bigfoot Hunters Are Seeking Evidence of Bigfoot in the Hawkeye State." *Daily Iowan*, December 8. 2020.

Roberts, James. "Iowa Bigfoot Sightings." Hangar 1 Publishing. https://hangar1publishing.com.

Weatherly, David. *Monsters of the Hawkeye State: Cryptids & Legends of Iowa (Monsters of America)*. Eerie Lights, 2022.

Lake and River Monsters

Clough, Eric. "Terror in Our Backyard: Four Monsters in Iowa." 97.7 FM KCRR, October 28, 2022.

Cryptid Wiki. "Obojoki." https://cryptidz.fandom.com/wiki.

It's Something. "Big Blue." https://itsmth.fandom.com/wiki.

Kay, Tiffany. "Iowa Monsters: Monster Turtle of Big Blue." K92.3, October 21, 2020.

Vulich, Nick. *Gruesome Iowa: Murder, Madness and the Macabre in the Hawkeye State*. Lulu, 2019.

The Metamorphosis Sculpture

Walters, Bruce. "Art in Plain Sight: Metamorphosis." *River Cities Reader*, August 2015.

UFOs in Iowa

Ackley Enterprise. "Strange Phenomenon." February 8, 1878.

Goldfield, Raymond. "UFO Was Sighted in Iowa 46 Years Ago and It's One of the Most Credible UFO Sightings in History." Only in Iowa, October 2, 2023. onlyiniowa.com.

Ground News. "'It Makes You Wonder': Iowa Father & Son Duo Find Crop Circles in Soybean Crop in 1996." groundnews.com.

Offutt, Jason. "Mass of Molten Metal Leaves Bystanders with Questions." Savannah Now, February 9, 2011. savannahnow.com.

Sioux City Journal. February 3, 1897, 3.

The St. Elizabeth Premonition

Daily Times. "Friends Tell of Mrs. Anna Neal's Prophecies of Tragedy." January 13, 1950.

Grimes, Bret. Interview by Michael McCarty, October 2024.

———. *The St. Elizabeth's Hospital Fire in Iowa*. The History Press, 2024.

Richard-Sloane Special Collections, Davenport Public Library. "The St. Elizabeth's Tragedy Part II of II." January 21, 2015.

Smith, Doug. Interview by Michael McCarty, October 2024.

Mars Hill Church

Got Questions. "What Happened at Mars Hill in the Bible." www.gotquestions.org/Mars-Hill.html.

Harness, Pearl Rupe. "Mars Hill Log Church." Annals of Iowa. pubs.lib.uiowa.edu/annals-of-iowa/article/10431/galley/119017/view.

Magaraci, Kim. "The History Behind This Log Cabin Church in Iowa Is Astounding." Only in Iowa. www.onlyinyourstate.com/stays/iowa/mars-hill-church-ia

WhisperWeb. "The Satanic Panic." Medium, January 10, 2023. medium.com/@whisperweb/the-satanic-panic-debefc28b29a.

Wikipedia. "Satanic Panic." wikipedia.com.

Earling Exorcism

Hauck, Dennis William. *Haunted Places: The National Directory: Ghostly Abodes, Sacred Sites, UFO Landings and Other Supernatural Locations*. Penguin 1994.

Hushed Up History. "Evil and Exorcism of Emma Schmidt." May 27, 2020. husheduphistory.com.

Laycock, Joseph P., ed. *The Penguin Book of Exorcisms*. Penguin Random House, 2020.

Rounds, Peg. Interview by Michael McCarty, December 2024.

Scott, Beth, and Michael Norman. *Haunted Heartland*. Dorset Press, 1985.

Steiger, Brad. *Real Ghosts, Restless Spirits and Haunted Places*. Visible Ink Press, 2003.

The Goddess of West Branch

Blavatsky, Helena. *Isis Unveiled: A Master-Key to the Mysteries of Ancient and Modern Science and Theology*. Theosophy Company, 1945.

Davis, Jenny Cripe. "Statue of Isis." National Park Service.

Herbert Hoover Presidential Library and Museum. National Archives.

Howard, Spencer. "Isis, the Wandering Goddess." National Archives. https://hoover.blogs.archives.gov.

Wikipedia. "Das verschleierte Bild zu Sais." wikipedia.com.

Mysterious Mounds of Iowa

Bannister, Megan. *Secret Iowa: A Guide to the Weird, Wonderful and Obscure*. Reedy Press, 2023.

Carlson, Jean. "Elegy for an Elephant: Oquawka Commemorates 50 Years Since the Death of Norma Jean." Tri States Public Radio, July 13, 2022.

Gaul, Alma. "Davenport City Cemetery Mystery Solved." *Quad City Times*, July 23, 2023.

Hancock, Graham. *Fingerprints of the Gods*. Crown, 1995.

Hantman, Jeffrey. "Jefferson's Mound Archaeological Site." *Encyclopedia Virginia*. Virginia Humanities.

Iowa Natural Heritage Foundation. "Explore Iowa: Effigy Mounds National Monument." https://www.inhf.org.

Kastell, Christina, Curator of History and Anthropology, Putnam Museum, Davenport. Interview with authors, summer of 2024.

McCarty, Michael, and Mark McLaughlin. *Ghosts of the Quad Cities*. The History Press, 2019.

McKusick, Marshall Bassford. *The Davenport Conspiracy Revisited*. River House Books, 1991.

Richard-Sloane Special Collections, Davenport Public Library. "April Fools, Not Us." April 1, 2008.

SCBlogger. "The Davenport Conspiracy." Selections for the Special Collections, Davenport Public Library.

Thomas Jefferson Encyclopedia. "Jefferson's Excavation of a Native American Burial Mound." Monticello, Virginia.

Whalen, Kathryn, Richard-Sloane Special Collections, Davenport Public Library. Interview with authors, summer of 2024.

Wikipedia. "Davenport Tablets." wikipedia.com.

———. "Graham Hancock." wikipedia.com.

Count Nicholas Fejervary

Walters, Bruce. "Buried Stories: Count Nicholas Fejervary, 1811–1895." *River Cities Reader*, January 2023.

Abandoned in Iowa

American Urbex. "Dubuque Brewing and Malting." americanurbex.com.

Cristy. "A Famous Mansion Was Built & Left to Decay in the Middle of an Iowa Cornfield." Only in Iowa, November 27, 2023. onlyiniowa.com.

Encyclopedia Dubuque. "Dubuque Brewing and Malting." encyclopediadubuque.com.

Gerlach, Kelly. "Buckhorn Rebirth: Former Creamery Revitalized for Construction, Salvage." *Maquoketa Sentinel-Press*, January 2, 2019.

Gorah, David. "10 Abandoned Ghost Towns in Iowa, United States—Pretty Cool and Creepy at the Same Time." *Vintage News*, December 3, 2015.

Hatch Developing Grout. "Dubuque Brewing and Malting." 2021. hatchdevelopinggrout.com.

International Movie Data Base (IMDB). "Tom Arnold." imdb.com.

Jackson County Historical Society. "Hurstville Lime Kilns." June 18, 2016.

Julien's Journal. "Trappist Caskets: The Dubuque Brewing and Malting Company." June 25, 2020. juliensjournal.com.

Mac, Kerri. "What Ever Happened to Roseanne Barr's Eldon Dinner?" K 92.3 FM, February 3, 2022.

McCarty, Michael, and John Brassard Jr. *Eerie Quad Cities*. The History Press, 2021.

Natalie. "This Terrifying Iowa Ghost Town Is Just 45 Minutes from the Quad Cities." B100 FM, October 3, 2017.

Silos & Smokestacks. https://www.silosandsmokestacks.org.

Tattoo Johnny. "Roseanne Barr Celebrity Tattoos." June 29, 2015. tattoojohnny.com.

TMZ. "Tom Arnold: Roseanne Tattoo Was the Worst Mistake of My Life." tmz.com.

Wikipedia. "Roseanne Barr." wikipedia.com.

Whatever Happened to Black Hawk's Remains?

Black Hawk. *Autobiography of Ma-Ka-Tai-Me-She-Kia-Kiak, or Black Hawk*. Edited by J.B. Patterson. J.B. Patterson, 1833.

Britannica. "Black Hawk War." britannica.com.

Carvey, Beth, retired director and historian of the Black Hawk State Historic Site. Interview by Michael McCarty, October 4, 2024.

Center for the History of Medicine. "The Fowler Brothers." Harvard Countway Library.

Dodd, Charles. "Reminiscences of Black Hawk." Central States Archaeological Journal 6, no. 1 (1959): 33–39.

Fry, Russ. "Does the University of Iowa Have Black Hawk's Remains?" CreateSpace Independent Publishing Platform, 2018.

Nossaman, Sarah Welch. "Pioneering at Bonaparte and Near Pella." Explorations in Iowa History Project, Northern Iowa University.

Ruger, Ruthhart. "Saukenuk Once Home to Black Hawk and More than 6,000 Sauk." *Moultrie County News Progress*, October 21, 2018.

Stevens, Frank Everett. *The Black Hawk War, Including a Review of Black Hawk's Life*. Self-published, 1903. Retrieved from the Library of Congress. https://www.loc.gov/item/03017803.

Trask, Kerry A. *The Battle of the Heart of America*. Henry Holt and Company, 2007.

Van Wyhe, John. "The History of Phrenology on the Web." historyofphrenology.org.uk.
Vulich, Nick. *Early Days in Davenport and Rock Island*. Lulu, 2021.

Ghosts

The Villisca Axe Murders

Bannister, Megan. *Secret Iowa: A Guide to the Weird, Wonderful and Obscure*. Reedy Press, 2023.
Barreda, Virginia. "What to Know on the Anniversary of the Villisca Ax Murders." *Des Moines Register*, June 9, 2022.
Epperly, Edgar V. *Fiend Incarnate: Villisca Axe Murders of 1912*. Independently published, 2021.
Iowa Cold Cases. iowacoldcases.org.
Pieces of Iowa's Past. "1912 Axe Murders in Villisca Remain Unsolved." May 13, 2015. https://www.legis.iowa.gov/docs/publications/TB/663533.pdf.
Rundle, Kelly. Interview by Bruce Walters and Michael McCarty, November 2024.
Terrifying Real-Life Stories Haunted Houses & Scary Mysteries. Hearst Specialist, 2024.
Vulich, Nick. *Spine-Chilling Murders in Iowa*. Independently published, 2021.

Wapsi Willy

Iowa Lincoln Highway Association. "Legend of Wapsi Willy." October 27, 2018. https://www.iowalincolnhighway.com.
Steen, Penni. Interview by Michael McCarty, November 2024.

The Ghost of Hazel

Templeman, Tara. "Cedar Rapids Ghost Stories: The Time Hazel McGrew's Ghost Was Spotted in the Library." *Gazette*, October 20, 2020.

Farrar Elementary School

Ames Tribune. "Ghost Hunters Look for Bumps in the Night at Old Farrar School." July 13, 2015.
Estep, Richard, and E.E. Benson. *A Haunting at Farrar*. Independently published, 2019.
Haunting at Farrar. https://www.facebook.com/HauntingAtFarrar.

Haunted Hospitals

Clough, Eliot. "A Haunted History Surrounds Like Mental Health Institute Near Waterloo, Iowa." 106.9 Kroc, October 19, 2021.

Edinburgh Manor. https://edinburghmanor.wixsite.com/edinburgh.

Grimes, Bret. Interview by Michael McCarty, October 2024.

Haunted Rooms Company. "Independence State Hospital." https://www.hauntedrooms.com.

Iowa PBS. "Local Legends Around Iowa 'Haunted' Locations." https://www.iowapbs.org.

Nielson, Chris. *Fear and Fascination in Edinburgh Manor*. Independently published, 2023.

———. Interview by Michael McCarty, September 2024.

Westhoff, Tory, and Josh Heard. *We Are Edinburgh Manor*. Lulu, 2021.

Haunted Hotels and Inns

Courtlin. "Stay the Night at One of Iowa's Haunted Hotels." 98.1 KHNK, October 16, 2024.

Cristy. "The Historic Hotel Ottumwa in Iowa Is Notoriously Haunted and We Dare You to Spend the Night." Only in Iowa, October 28, 2021. onlyiniowa.com.

Distilled Opinion. "1846 Mason House Inn, Bentonsport, Iowa: History and Ghosts." August 26, 2017. distilledopinion.com.

Haunted Houses. "Dubuque, Iowa, Hotel Julien." https://hauntedhouses.com.

Haunted Rooms Company. "The 50 Most Haunted Hotels in America." hauntedrooms.com.

Hotel Ottumwa. https://www.hotelottumwa.com.

Kresol, Kathi. "Rambling Along the Mississippi—Dubuque, Iowa." Haunted Rockford, July 17, 2017. hauntedrockford.com.

Kristin. "The Most Haunted Places in Iowa." Let's Roam, September 12, 2023.

Magaraci, Kim. "The Oldest Hotel in Iowa Is Also One of the Most Haunted Places You'll Sleep." Only in Iowa, January 17, 2019. onlyiniowa.com.

———. "This 173-Year-Old Inn Is One of the Most Haunted Places in Iowa… and You Can Spend the Night." Only in Iowa, June 29, 2019. onlyiniowa.com.

Mason House Inn. "Ghostly Encounters." masonhouseinn.com.

Haunted Cemeteries

Brassard, John, Jr. "Defiling the Dead." October 17, 2017. johnbrassardjr.com.

———. "Desecration: Cemetery Vandalism and Grave Robbery." March 26, 20217. johnbrassardjr.com.

———. "Unfinished Business: Walking the Rows of Iowa's Haunted Cemeteries." October 14, 2020. johnbrassardjr.com.

G-Hunter. "Pleasant Ridge Cemetery: 13 Steps." https://g-hunter.tripod.com/id20.html.

Hauck, Dennis William. *Haunted Places: The National Directory: Ghostly Abodes, Sacred Sites, UFO Landings and Other Supernatural Locations*. Penguin, 1994.

Iowa PBS. "Iowa's Unique Gravestones and Burials." https://www.iowapbs.org.

JT. "Iowa Legends and Ghost Stories: 13 Steps." October 12, 2020. B100.com.

Lewis, Chad, and Kevin Nelson. "Do Not Touch the Gate at the Haunted Hickory Hill Cemetery." YouTube channel "Supernatural Dares," October 24, 2019.

Palos Chambers of Commerce. paloschambersofcommerce.com.

Paulson, D. "These 10 Haunted Cemeteries in Iowa Are Not for the Faint of Heart." Only in Iowa, August 7, 2016. onlyiniowa.com.

Templeman, Tara. "History Behind the 'Haunted' Tillie in Cedar Rapids, Marion." *Gazette*, September 20, 2021.

Times-Republican. "Paranormal Iowa." June 13, 2015.

Trautmann, Mike. "Here's 170 Haunted Places in Iowa to Make You Shiver." *Des Moines Register*, October 23, 2024.

Eerie Angel Statues

"Ghoul Guide." 106.5 FM. https://big1065.iheart.com/featured/qc-ghoul-guide.

Haunted Places. "Greenwood Cemetery." hauntedplaces.com.

Omaha Exploration. "Audrey Munson and the Black Angel." December 20, 2023. https://omahaexploration.com.

Orngard, Shellie. "Here Stands the Ruth Anne Dodge Memorial Known as the Black Angel." Prairie Rivers of Iowa.

Trollinger, Vernon. *Haunted Iowa City*. The History Press, 2011.

Wikipedia. "Ruth Anne Dodge Memorial." https://en.wikipedia.org.

Williamson, Zach. "The History, and Haunting, of Council Bluffs' Black Angel." KMTV.

Terror Bridges

Atlas Obscura. "Lover's Leap Swinging Bridge, Columbus Junction, Iowa." atlasobsura.com.

Bannister, Megan. *Secret Iowa: A Guide to the Weird, Wonderful and Obscure*. Reedy Press, 2023.

Iowa Department of Transportation. https://iowadot.gov.
Madison County, Iowa Chamber of Commerce. https://www.madisoncounty.com.
Monti, Ruth Ann. "One of the Most Haunted Bridges in Iowa Has Been Around Since the 1800s." Only in Iowa, October 7, 2023. onlyiniowa.com.
Patrick, Kirk. "Dare to Cross the Haunted Bridge in Iowa Known as Lover's Leap." 97.7 KCPK, January 13, 2022.
Paulson, D. "The Story Behind This Haunted Iowa Bridge Will Give You Nightmares." Only in Iowa. onlyiniowa.com.
Poll, Mary Ann. "Haunted Destinations: The Banwell Terror Bridge." Medium, October 14, 2021.
Webb, Emily. "Notorious Haunted Bridge in Iowa Spooks Visitors Since 1800s." Y105, October 18, 2021.

Haunted Museums and Art Galleries

"Ashes to Ashes: Iowa's First Cremation." Primary Selections from the Davenport Public Library Special Collections, March 13, 2021.
Atlas Obscura. "Mississippi Spoon Gallery." atlasobsura.com.
City of Dakota City, Iowa. https://www.dakotacityiowa.com.
City of Dubuque. https://cityofdubuque.org.
Cook, Linda. "Father Conroy's of Hope Serves Its Last Meal." *Quad City-Times*, September 24, 2019.
Davenport Tribune. March 12, 1891.
Force, Philip. Interview by Michael McCarty, November 2024.
Gaul, Alma. "Sister Ludmilla Is Driving Spirit at Father's Conroy of Hope." *Quad-City Times*, December 25, 2011.
German American Heritage Center & Museum Facebook page. Post from October 22, 2023. https://www.facebook.com/gahc712.
Ghosts of America. "Dakota City, Iowa Ghost Sightings." https://www.ghostsofamerica.com.
"Ghoul Guide." 106.5 FM. https://big1065.iheart.com/featured/qc-ghoul-guide.
Harvey, Jolene. Interview by Michael McCarty, November 2024.
McCarty, Michael, and Kristin DeMarr. *Quad Cities Beer: A History*. The History Press, 2023.
National Mississippi River Museum and Aquarium. https://www.rivermuseum.org.
Painter, Sally. "10 Haunted Places to Visit in Iowa for Ghost Enthusiasts." Love to Know, August 20, 2021. lovetoknow.com.
Richard-Sloane Special Collections, Davenport Public Library.
S., Marla. "Dubuque Is Allegedly One of Iowa's Most Haunted Small Towns." Only in Your State, updated September 26, 2022. https://www.onlyinyourstate.com.

Tobin, Clare. Interview by Bruce Walters, January 2025.

———. Interview by Michael McCarty, November 2024.

Trautmann, Mike. "Get Spooked with Iowa Ghost Stories." *Des Moines Register*, October 24, 2022.

Turner, Jonathan. "Davenport Woman Aims for Upon Collection Record." Our Quad Cities, April 18, 2023. ourquadcities.com.

Wikipedia. "German American Heritage Center." wikipedia.com.

Willard, John. "An Acceptable Way of Death." *Quad-City Times*, November 21, 1976.

Haunted Jails

Delaney, Robin. "From Mental Health Facility to Prison: Warren Tells of Mount Pleasant Prison." *Daily Gate City*, May 21, 2024.

Erinn, Dani. "The Serial Killer Who Killed Over 44 People Believes His Name Is a Hex." Medium.

Historical Society of Pottawattamie County. Squirrel Cage Jail Museum.

Historic Iowa State Penitentiary Inc. October 26, 2022.

Iowa Department of Corrections. "Mount Pleasant." https://doc.iowa.gov.

Iowa's History Journal. "Unlocking Time Behind Bars: Escapes, Executes and Reforms at Fort Madison Old State Penitentiary." https://iowahistoryjournal.com.

McClary, Daryl C. "Police Capture Serial Killer Jake Bird After He Murders Two Tacoma Women on October 30." October 5, 2006. Available at https://www.historylink.org/File/7971.

Midwest Wanderer. "Touring the Haunted Squirrel Cage Jail Museum." https://midwestwanderer.com.

North Central Correctional Facility Annual Report, 2019.

Trautmann, Mike. "Here's 170 Haunted Places in Iowa to Make You Shiver." *Des Moines Register*, October 23, 2024.

"Welcome to the Historic Squirrel Cage Jail." Flyer and information displayed in the Squirrel Cage Jail Museum.

John Looney and Ghosts

Awesome Stories. "John & Connor Looney." http://media.awesomestories.com.

Dillon, Tom. "The King of Rock Island (Part 3): One Murder Too Many Starts Looney's Downfall." *Observer* (Augustana College), October 15, 1975.

Hammer, Richard, and Roger Ruthhart. *Citadel of Sin: The John Looney Story*. Moline Dispatch Publishing Company, 2007.

McCarty, Michael. *Esoteria-Land*. BearManor Media, 2009.
McCarty, Michael, and Mark McLaughlin. *Ghosts of the Quad Cities*. The History Press, 2019.
Vulich, Nick. *Early Days in Davenport and Rock Island*. Lulu, 2021.
Wundram, Bill. "Murder, Chaos Ruled in Bloody Looney Era." *Quad-City Times*, July 7, 2002.

A Little Eerie

Iowa's TV Horror Hosts

Naumann, Scott. Interview by Michael McCarty, December 2024.

Iowa's Conservationist and the Devil's Tower Connection

Plaque at the Lacey-Keosauqua State Park.

Stony Hollow Road

Kendall, Michael. "These 10 Urban Legends in Iowa Will Keep You Awake at Night." Only in Iowa, July 2, 2015. onlyiniowa.com.
Magaraci, Kim. "The Mysterious Iowa Road You Absolutely Must Drive at Least Once." Only in Iowa, October 18, 2022. onlyiniowa.com.

Cresco Opera House

Cresco Theatre & Opera House. https://www.crescotheatreoperahouse.com.
Cresco Times. "The Theme 'Pedal to the Paranormal.'" July 26, 2017.
Goldfield, Raymond. "The Haunted Theater in Iowa Both History Buffs and Ghost Hunters Will Love." Only in Iowa, September 9, 2022. onlyiniowa.com.
Trautmann, Mike. "Here's 170 Haunted Places in Iowa to Make You Shiver." *Des Moines R*egister, October 23, 2024.
Travel Iowa. "13 of Iowa's Most Haunted." https://www.traveliowa.com.

The Future Home of Captain Kirk

Atlas Obscura. atlasobsura.com.
Bannister, Megan. *Secret Iowa: A Guide to the Weird, Wonderful and Obscure*. Reedy Press, 2023.

Halloween: 25 Years of Terror. Directed and co-written by Stefan Hutchinson, 2006.

Ibrahim, Samantha. "William Shatner Rips *Halloween* for Using Captain Kirk Mask: 'Are They Kidding?'" *New York Post*, October 10, 2021.

Rushing, Ty. "Iowa Weird: How Riverside Became the Home of Captain Kirk." Starting Line, 2022. https://iowastartingline.com.

Star Trek. "Was Michael Myers' Halloween Mask William Shatner's Face?" startrek.com.

The Voyage Home Museum, Riverside History Center. https://www.voyagehomemuseum.org.

Wikipedia. "James T. Kirk." wikipedia.com.

ABOUT THE AUTHORS

Photo by Bruce Walters.

Professor Emeritus BRUCE WALTERS has taught at Western Illinois University, Marycrest College in Davenport and Augustana College in Rock Island. He has annually exhibited Halloween artworks since 2007, including artworks at the Des Moines Art Center, Des Moines, and the Figge Art Museum, Davenport, as well as in solo exhibitions at Quad City Arts Center, Rock Island, Illinois; the Western Illinois Art Gallery, Macomb, Illinois; the Contemporary Art Center, Peoria, Illinois; the Creative Arts Academy, Davenport; Black Hawk College, Moline, Illinois; and the German American Heritage Center and Museum, Davenport. As a graphic designer and illustrator, Walters has created life-size paintings for permanent display at the Hauberg Museum for the Illinois Historic Preservation Agency, displayed in Millennium Park in Chicago, and political cartoons for the *Quad City Times*' editorial page; designed websites; and created artwork for book covers. Walters has written columns and feature articles, including "Buried Stories" and "Art in Plain Sight," for the *River Cities Reader*. He is married to his wife, Laurie, and has three grown children. For additional information on him and his achievements, visit en.wikipedia.org/wiki/Bruce_Walters.

Michael McCarty in a graveyard. *Courtesy John Brassard Jr.*

MICHAEL MCCARTY has been a professional writer since 1983 and is the author of more than fifty books of fiction and nonfiction. His nonfiction includes *Ghosts of the Quad Cities* (with Mark McLaughlin), *Eerie Quad Cities* (with John Brassard Jr.), *Quad Cities Beer: A History* (with Kristin DeMarr), *Estoria-Land*, *Modern Mythmakers: 35 Interviews with Horror and Science Fiction Writers and Filmmakers* and *More Modern Mythmakers*. His fiction includes *Frankenstein's Mistress: Tales of Love & Monsters*, *Dracula Transformed and Other Bloodthirsty Tales*, *Dark Duets*, *Dark Cities: Dark Tales*, *A Little Help from My Fiends*, *Liquid Diet & Midnight Snack*, *Lost Girl of the Lake*, *Biters: Tales of Zombies & Vampires*, *Laughing in the Dark*, *I Kissed a Ghoul*, *Waiting for the Night* and the science fiction kid's book *Rusty the Robot's Holiday Adventures*. He is a five-time Bram Stoker Finalist and in 2008 won the David R. Collins Literary Achievement Award from the Midwest Writing Center. He lives in Rock Island, Illinois, with his wife, Cindy, and pet rabbit, Yeti. His blog site is http://monstermikeyaauthor.wordpress.com. Like his official Facebook page at http://www.facebook.com/michaelmccarty.horror.